George Washington Patten

Voices of the Border

George Washington Patten

Voices of the Border

ISBN/EAN: 9783337341992

Printed in Europe, USA, Canada, Australia, Japan

Cover: Foto ©Thomas Meinert / pixelio.de

More available books at **www.hansebooks.com**

VOICES OF THE BORDER;

COMPRISING

SONGS OF THE FIELD, SONGS OF THE BOWER, INDIAN MELODIES, AND PROMISCUOUS POEMS.

BY

LT. COL. G. W. PATTEN,

UNITED STATES ARMY.

"I have song of war for knight;
Lay of love for ladye bright."
Wandering Harper.

NEW YORK:
PUBLISHED BY HURD AND HOUGHTON,
459 BROOME STREET.
1867.

Entered according to Act of Congress, in the year 1867, by
G. W. PATTEN,
in the Clerk's Office of the District Court for the Southern District of New York.

RIVERSIDE, CAMBRIDGE:
STEREOTYPED AND PRINTED BY
H. O. HOUGHTON AND COMPANY.

To
LIEUTENANT-GENERAL WINFIELD SCOTT,

THE GREAT PACIFICATOR,

SUCH PORTION OF THIS VOLUME AS IS COMPRISED IN THE
"SONGS OF THE FIELD" WAS ORIGINALLY INSCRIBED,
AS A SLIGHT TESTIMONIAL OF THE HIGH ESTEEM
ENTERTAINED FOR THE DISTINGUISHED
STRATEGIST, BY HIS FRIEND AND
COMRADE IN ARMS,

THE AUTHOR.

NEW YORK CITY, *April,* 1867.

In presenting the subjoined poems to the reader, the writer is actuated principally by the motive of rescuing from literary shipwreck some of his fugitive pieces, which hitherto have floated, rudderless, on the uncertain current of the public press.

Having been stationed for many years at the frontier posts of the country, it might reasonably be supposed that the pen to him would be less familiar than the sword. Yielding, however, to the frequent solicitations of his friends, he has consented to arrange for them a full bouquet of those flowers which presented, hitherto, singly, have been received with a smile of favor, if not by an expression of regard.

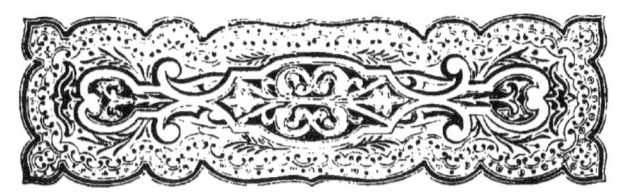

CONTENTS.

SONGS OF THE FIELD.

	PAGE
SONG OF THE SWORD	17
THE AMERICAN BIVOUAC ON THE BANK OF THE RIO GRANDE	20
LANDING OF THE FIRST AMERICAN LINE AT VERA CRUZ	23
THE LADY OF VERA CRUZ	26
THE VICTOR'S DREAM	29
THE SOLDIER'S DIRGE	31
SONG OF THE FIELD	32
LINES ON THE BURIAL OF A WEST POINT CADET	34
WAR SONG OF ERIN	36
WAR SONG OF FREEDOM	37
THE DEAD WARRIOR	38
THE ASSEMBLY	40
THE WARRIOR BARD	41
SONG OF THE DRAGOON	42
THE WAR-DRUM	43
THE ARMY IN THE FIELD	47
THE TRUMPET	49
LINES ON A DECEASED COMRADE	51
THE DREAM OF BATTLE	53
SONG OF THE WRECKER	55
THE DYING VOLUNTEER	57
LANDING OF THE FLORIDA REGULARS AT TAMPA BAY	60
THE WASTE WORN	62
BOYHOOD	64
THE TWO VOICES	66
THE SOLDIER'S VISION	69

CONTENTS.

	PAGE
THE SOLDIER'S REQUIEM	72
COME, LET US DIE LIKE MEN	74
THE WIND SPIRIT	76
THE GATHERING	80
SONG OF THE YOUNG SCOUT	82
THE YOUNG WARRIOR	84

SONGS OF THE BOWER.

THE DREAMING BOY	89
THOU HAST WOOED ME WITH PLEDGES	99
SHE WROTE	100
STANZAS FOR MUSIC	101
THOU WERT NOT THERE	102
MIDNIGHT	103
THE EYE OF CERULEAN BLUE	104
LOVE AND REASON	106
I CANNOT LOVE HER	109
THE ISLE OF LOVE	111
BURNING LETTERS	113
STANZAS	115
VENUS OF CANOVA	117
TO IANTHE	119
I LIVE FOR THEE	120
THE DYING BETROTHED	121
IGNORANCE AND BEAUTY	123
FALSE GAYETY	124
THE RESTLESS ONE	125
THE CHILD'S REQUIEM	127
THE RETURN	128
IMPROMPTU	129
THE LORE OF LOVE	130
THE LORE OF TEARS	132
THE OUTCAST	134
THE DISCARDED	136
LOVE'S PERFIDY	138
ROSALIE	140

CONTENTS.

	PAGE
FRAGMENT	143
THE DYING PENITENT	144
THE FOREVER LOST	145
MATILDA	147
THE DESERTED BRIDE	149
THE DEAD MOTHER	151
THE LUTE AND SHELL	154
I COME TO THY PRESENCE	155
MY BOSOM IS A SEPULCHRE	156
THE RED ROSE ; OR, PRIDE REPROVED	157
STANZAS FOR MUSIC	159
THE EAGLE AND DOVE	160
THE BRIDE'S PRAYER	162
DREAM OF THE BETROTHED	164
TO ADA	166
THE CONSTANT ONE	168
THE LAST LOOK	170
THE MAIDEN'S HEART	172
THE SCARCE FORGOTTEN	173
STANZAS	175
THE LONELY GRAVE	177
FOREVER THINE	179
SHE LOVES ANOTHER	180
STANZAS	181
STANZAS TO MARY	183
DEATH OF THE IMPROVISATRICE	186
THE CLOUD AND STREAM	190
COME WHERE THE BILLOW HEAVES	191
SONG	192
COME THOU AT NIGHT	193
THE MANIAC'S VISION	194
OH, BLAME HER NOT	196
SONNET TO THE OCEAN	197
CHERISHED TOKENS	198
CHIDE MILDLY THE ERRING	200
THE COTTAGE GIRL	201
THE DEATH OF MARY	203
UNREQUITED LOVE	205
THE RETORT	206

CONTENTS.

	PAGE
SERENADE	207
FIRST LOVE	208
HYMN FOR LILLA	209
THE WREATH YOU TWINED	210
LIFE DREAMS	211
MEASURE FOR MUSIC	213
LOVE AND THE LILY	214
LINES TO E——	216
STANZAS	217
NEVER MORE	219
WHAT SHALL I TELL HER	220
TWILIGHT STANZAS	222
BEAUTY SLEEPING	223
AND THOU WERT FALSE	224
CAUTION	226
ALEIDA	227
SOFTLY THE SENTRY STARS OF NIGHT	229
I WILL NOT LEAVE THEE NOW	230
I EVER DREAM OF THEE	231
THE UNREGRETTED	232
MARY'S LIPS ARE RED WITH ROSES	233
LATTICE PEEPING	234
THINK NOT THAT I LOVE THEE	236
WHY DOTH MUSIC CHARM NO MORE	237
THE UNREQUITED	238
THE GRAVE OF MELLON	240
THE BRIDE'S DEPARTURE	242
THE PASSING BELL	244
THE RELEASED SPIRIT	246
PRAYER OF THE YOUNG NOVICE	248
BRIDE UPON THY MARRIAGE DAY	249
SUNBEAMS AND SHADOWS	251
FLOWERS AND POETRY FOR ADA	253
THE AGED MOTHER	254
LINES AT MY SISTER'S GRAVE	256
DEATH OF ADA	258
I'M STANDING BY THEE, FATHER DEAR	261
THE PAST	263

INDIAN MELODIES.

	PAGE
THE SEMINOLE'S REPLY	267
TA-BISE-QUONGH	270
PAWNEE LOVE-SONG	272
PAWNEE CURSE	274
SONG OF THE TRAIL	276
SONG OF THE INDIAN GIRL	278
SONG OF THE EMIGRANT INDIAN	280
INDIAN DIRGE	282
NIGHT ON THE SANTA FÉ, FLORIDA	284
SONG OF THE "CRIMSON HAND"	287
PALE EVE ON WING OF STARLIGHT RAYS	291
INDIAN MELODY	295
THE FLIGHT	297
THE FALL OF MONIAC	299
THE MISTAKEN VOLUNTEER	302
SONG OF THE OKEE-FEE-NOKEE	305

PROMISCUOUS POEMS.

THE POWERS OF WOMAN	313
THE CALIFORNIA TRANSPORT	316
THE BRIDE'S LAST SLEEP	319
CHANGE	320
THE CONDEMNED CHRISTIAN	322
THE OCEAN	325
DESULTORY RHYMES	328
CAROLINE OF ENGLAND	331
THE HYMN OF DEATH	335
THE IMP OF THE PALACE	337
SONG OF THE SEA	340
THE NEGLECTED OPPORTUNITY	342
IN MEMORIAM	344
THE WINTRY WRECK	346
GOING HOME	348
THE MERRY SLEIGH	350

	PAGE
THE LOVER'S LEASE	352
THE LOST CREED	354
LOVE'S PERFIDY	356
THE FOOT-RACE	358
RHYMES FOR THE TIMES	359

SONGS OF THE FIELD.

"And there was mounting in hot haste." — *Byron.*

VOICES OF THE BORDER.

SONG OF THE SWORD.

SWORD! which sleepeth in thy sheath,
Hear'st thou not the trumpet's breath,
Where the column deep with death,
    Tarries for thy crest?
Know'st thou not the lot is thine,
Glist'ning in the sun to shine,
Foremost mid the forming line?
    Wake thee from thy rest!

Sword! that doth in darkness lie,
Girded fast unto my thigh,
See'st thou not 'gainst yonder sky
    Banners sweeping low?
Never thus may'st thou remain,
Yield thee to my hand again,
For the tear of crimson stain
    Down thy cheek must flow.

Sword! when first thy glittering light
Flashed athwart my youthful sight,
Playfully I called thee bright
  As an angel's form.
Years have passed, nor yet we part,
Thou art wedded to my heart,
Though I often feel thou art
  Dreadful as the storm.

Sword! although thy bosom's sheen
'Broidered be and polished keen,
Wheresoe'er its glow is seen
  Shadowed 't is with fears.
Though thy glance seems mild and meek,
Such as Love's own eyes might speak,
Yet the smile will leave the cheek
  Where its light appears.

Sword! I deeply love thy ray,
'T is to me the light of day,
Yet, oh yet, thou tak'st away,
  Bridegroom from the bride.
Pointing upward to the star,
On the crest of Glory's car,
Thou dost urge to fields of war
  Breaking hearts allied.

Sword! though fearful be thy gift,
Once again thy blade I lift,

O'er my steed, a meteor swift,
    Flashing shalt thou wave.
Thou shalt strike in many wars,
Battle for thy country's laws,
Thou shalt plead the orphan's cause
    O'er the patriot's grave.

Sword of beauty! sword of fear!
Shoutings mad are on my ear;
Steel! where art thou? *thou art here,* —
    Faithful to the last.
Mid the battle's heartless hum,
Mid the rolling of the drum,
Cry "Huzza!" I come — *we* come,
    Rushing like the blast!

THE AMERICAN BIVOUAC ON THE BANK OF THE RIO GRANDE, IN THE YEAR 1846.

A SONG went up, at the close of day,
From the shining land where the gold-mines lay;
Strangely, the while, mid citrons ripe,
Glistened the flag of the star and stripe.
There were foreign bands in the sunset light,
Lying at ease with their falchions bright,
And they lifted their heads the vines among,
At the thrilling sounds of their native tongue.

"'T is glorious, — Oh, 't is glorious!"
 (Glad voices swelled the lay,)
"The flag amid the citron-trees,
 And the trumps that wake the day;
The lances bathed in liquid light,
 And the steeds that sweep the plain;
'T is glorious, — Oh, 't is glorious!
 On to the charge again!"

"But 't is lonely, — Oh, 't is lonely,"
 (A voice desponding sighed.)
"That we should leave our peaceful hearth
 For the battle's stormy tide;

That we should change for language strange
    Fond words we understand!
'T is lonely, — Oh, 't is lonely, —
    This march through foreign land."

"Nay, glorious, — Oh, 't is glorious!"
    (Rang that exulting cry,)
"To mark the floating of the stripes
    Amid the battle sky!
Beside the eagle's glistening crest,
    To watch its proud career,
And with an arm *above* the rest,
    To strike mid shout and cheer."

"'T is lonely, — Oh, 't is lonely,"
    (Still sighed that yearning heart,)
"All day we hear the roll that tells
    How human hopes depart;[*]
Lo! cross his hands upon his breast
    Which beat, like yours, for fame,
And bear him to his place of rest, —
    A grave without a name."

And the song was hushed on the evening breeze,
As the day grew dim through the plantain-trees;

---

[*] That more perished by sickness than by the sword, during the sojourn of the American army in Mexico, is a fact too well substantiated to be refuted. Accidentally passing, one morning, the hospital at Camargo, the author counted the remains of eight soldiers, who had died the night previous, placed side by side on the portico of the building, awaiting interment.

And the brows which were lit by the sunset west,
On the palm-leaf pillows drooped down in rest,
Some to recall their native sky —
Some to dream of *victory*.

<small>Camp near the Rio Grande,
December, 1846.</small>

LANDING OF THE FIRST AMERICAN LINE AT VERA CRUZ,

MARCH 9, 1847.

[At the signal "Land," telegraphed from the flagship of the commanding general, the surf-boats, which had been previously freighted with the troops of the first line, consisting of several regiments of artillery, approached the shore. They were covered by light-draughted gunboats anchored in the immediate vicinity of the beach. Meanwhile, as if for her own amusement, the inimitable little steamer *Spitfire*, commanded by the intrepid Captain Tatnell, shipped her anchor, rounded to, and threw her shells at the great Castle of San Juan d'Ulloa, like a child at play casting its marbles at the fortress of a giant. The castle roared back an angry reply, but did not succeed in inflicting any punishment upon the tantalizing aggressor.

Soon a prolonged shout from the " Army afloat " announced the unfurling of the American flag on the enemy's shore, where the excited soldiery were seen dashing from the boats, unmindful of the surf, in their earnestness to form and rally around the Star-spangled Banner.]

THE signal-flag is in the sky!
Ten thousand hearts are beating high!
Ye of the foremost line, draw nigh;
     Huzza!
" Prepare to land!" — take heed — stand by!
     Huzza!

The surf-boats touch the ship's tall side,
Along the lee they smoothly ride;
Impatient waits the gallant guide;
     Huzza!
Down, down, descend with rapid stride!
     Huzza!

Ye gallant men of hardy brow,
With bosoms like the lava's flow,
Be calm, be cool as winter's snow!
     Huzza!
Crowd close, sit down from stern to prow!
     Huzza!

See yonder fleet stretched out supine
From east to day's remote decline!
What voices cheer, what bright blades shine!
     Huzza!
Their eyes are on ye! form the line!
     Huzza!

Now watch the war-words once again!
All eyes upon the flag-ship's main!
" Land!" reads the signal, " land " — 't is plain —
     Huzza!
Cast off, give way with stalwart strain!
     Huzza!

Trim, trim the boat; ply, ply the oar —
The billows rave, the war-dogs roar —

The death-shells burst behind — before —
     Huzza!
Bend to the stroke, strain for the shore —
     Huzza!

The sea-walls shake with thunder riven!
Around ye War's red bolts are driven!
Above ye floats the bird of heaven!
     Huzza!
Strive, brothers, as ye ne'er have striven!
     Huzza!

The foremost surf-boat nears the land —
She grounds — out dash the dauntless band;
Follow, my boys, with flag in hand —
     Huzza!
We breast the surf, we gain the sand —
     Huzza!

Now raise the starry banner high —
Rally — close up — crowd round — stand by!
Our eagle rules the Aztec sky;
     Huzza!
Comrades, one cheer for victory!
     Huzza!

 Steamer "Eudora," off Vera Cruz,
  March 9, 1847.

THE LADY OF VERA CRUZ.

[DURING the three days' bombardment of the city of Vera Cruz by the American forces, in the month of March, 1847, the Mexican General Morelles, commanding at the Castle of San Juan d'Ulloa, which overlooks the city, was repeatedly applied to by the inhabitants of the town to surrender that stronghold, to prevent further effusion of blood, but without success; and the terrified citizens were awaiting, in despair, the advent of the storming column, hourly expected, which would desolate their sanctuaries and dye their hearthstones still deeper with the hue of slaughter, when, suddenly, a flag of truce was seen flaunting from the turret of the castle.

Active demonstrations immediately ceased, and the signal for a parley was sounded. The result of this conference was the surrender both of the castle and city, thus saving the inhabitants of the beleaguered town from an experience of the final ordeal of arms which they so much dreaded. It was rumored, at the time, that this unexpected acquiescence on the part of the commandant of the fortress with the wishes of the inhabitants of the city, was owing to the sickness of General Morelles, who had temporarily transferred his authority to a subordinate but more considerate officer.]

"STAY, soldier, stay — one kind reply —
   One answer to my soul's despair!
When will the death-shell cease to fly,
   The bullet hurtle through the air?
See, yonder, how the rockets gleam —
   The toppling steeples fall around —
And pouring thick its sulphurous stream,
   The belching howitz plows the ground."

"Lady! away — where sleeps thy pride?
    Thy gallant lord directs the field;
Art thou a true Castilian's bride,
    And yet would'st bid our leader yield?
We go to face the iron hail,
    Morelles! is our battle-cry,
One cause is ours — no heart must quail —
    'Morelles! — death or victory!'"

"I know my lord sustains the fight,
    And know his hand will do its best;
But tell him mid the strife to-night,
    His babe lies wounded on my breast.
Behold! is 't not a gentle child?
    Once with its locks he loved to play;
Last eve within his arms it smiled —
    He kissed it as he rode away;

"But now, alas! it smiles no more,
    Its cheek is pale and wild its brain;
See here! its robes are dark with gore —
    Soldier! — and must I plead in vain?
He hears me not — man scorns to hear
    Or mother's wail or infant's cry —
And hark! — again that dreadful cheer!
    'Morelles! — death or victory!'"

She sank before the image dim,
    Of her to earth a God who gave:

"Mother! through thee I plead to Him —
   Son of the Virgin! Jesu, save!"
Straight rings a trumpet on the blast,
   The "parley" sounds upon the air,
Up runs the white flag to the mast:
   Indulgent Heaven has heard her prayer.

CAMP BEFORE VERA CRUZ,
   27th *March*, 1847.

THE VICTOR'S DREAM.

[SUGGESTED on reading a paragraph in a city paper to the purport that the veteran Commander-in-Chief (Lieut. General Scott), soon after his return from Mexico, was observed to have dropped, apparently, into a slight doze, during the performance of divine service in one of the cathedrals.]

He sleeps! his brow of care
   Upon his hand is prest;
Unconscious of the public stare,
The heart, whose burdens few could bear,
   At length consents to rest.

Closed are the victor's eyes!
   Soften the organ's strain!
He dreams; hush! hark! his spirit flies,
On clouded wings of crimson dyes,
   To Cerro Gordo's plain.

For him revives once more
   The battle's glorious hour,
He hears the cannon's thunder roar,
And sees, afar, the red rain pour
   From stern D'Ulloa's tower.

He waves his flaming brand
   On Cherubusco's height,

And where, amid his chosen band,
Chapultepec, against his hand,
  In vain arrays her might;

Again the gauntlet flings
  At the old Aztec walls,
While fierce and far the war-cry rings,
Deep echoed from the "Mill of Kings,"*
  To Montezuma's halls.

Shattered beneath his blows
  Yawns the *Garita* wide,
While calmly, where the life-stream flows,
Stands, like a prince above his foes,
  The victor in his pride.

He sleeps! chant soft the air!
  Shut out the sunlight's gleam!
See on his brow the lines of care —
Breathe low! for him is slumber rare —
  Break not the conqueror's dream.

          * Molino del Rey.

THE SOLDIER'S DIRGE.

"Toll not the bell of death for me
When I am dead."

Oh! toll no bell
    When I am gone.
Let not a bugle swell
The mournful tale to tell;
 But let the drum
With hollow roll,
 Tell when the angels come
To take my soul:
And let the banner, borne before me,
Wave in azure glory o'er me,
    When I am gone.

Oh! shed no tear
    When I am gone.
Unmanly 't is to hear
Sobs at a soldier's bier;
 But let the peal,
Solemn and slow,
 From minute-gun reveal,
That I am low:
And with no costly pomp deride me,
But lean on arms reversed beside me,
    When I am gone.

SONG OF THE FIELD.

Roll! roll! How gladly swell the distant notes,
From where on high yon streaming pennon floats!
   Roll! roll! On gorgeously they come,
With plumes low stooping on their winding way,
And lances glancing in the sun's bright ray.
What do ye there, my merry comrades, say?
   We beat the gathering drum:
'T is this which gives to mirth a lighter tone,
To the young soldier's cheek a deeper glow;
When stretched upon his grassy couch alone,
It steals upon his ear — this martial call
Prompts him to dream of merry war, with all
     Its pageantry and show.

Roll! roll! What is it that ye beat?
  We sound the charge — on with the courser fleet!
Where amid columns red War's eagles fly,
     We swear to do or die.
'T is this which feeds the fires of Fame with breath,
Which steels the soldier's heart to deeds of death,
     And when his hand,
Fatigued with slaughter, pauses o'er the slain,
'T is this which prompts him madly once again
     To seize the bloody brand.

Roll! roll! Brothers, what do ye here.
Slowly and sadly as ye pass along,
With your dull march and low funereal song?
   Comrade, we bear a bier!
   I saw him fall:
And as he lay beneath his steed, methought,
(Strange how the mind such fancy should have
  wrought)
That had he died beneath his native skies,
Perchance some gentle bride had closed his eyes,
   And wept beside his pall.

LINES ON THE BURIAL OF A WEST POINT CADET.

I stood beside him while the sun
    Was sinking in the west,
Pouring its fading beams upon
    Banner and glittering crest.
Save from his cheek no passers by
    His boyhood could discern,
For martial fire was in his eye,
    His brow like manhood stern.

I stood beside him, and I drew
    A veil of gauze away;
His eyes were closed, cold clammy dew
    Upon his forehead lay.
Around his form I saw them twine
    A shroud in many a fold;
I took his listless hand in mine —
    'T was cold — 't was icy cold.

I stood beside him when they bore
    His body to the tomb;
Waving amid the train I saw
    Banner and bending plume.

Onward they moved with voices dumb,
  To music slow and drear:
Heavily rolled the muffled drum,
  Heavily groaned the bier.

I stood beside him, when they lowered
  His coffin in the ground,
I heard the grating of the cord,
  The falling clods resound.
I saw his comrades round him stand,
  The parting looks they gave;
I heard the voice of low command, —
  The volley o'er the grave.

I stood above him while the sun
  Was sinking in the west;
I saw a stone engraved upon,
  To mark his place of rest.
I saw the long grass waving high,
  I heard the wind's deep moan,
It seemed to whisper with a sigh,
  He sleeps alone, — alone.

WAR SONG OF ERIN.

Children of Erin, come forth from your mountains!
  The track of the Lord of the Desert is there,
He hath trod on your altars, polluted your fountains,
  Come, kneel at the feet of the Virgin and swear
    By the dark cloud of battle,
      Which hangs round the foe,
    By the hollow death-rattle,'
      Where bolt leaves the bow,
To sheathe not the steel till the spoiler shall flee
From the land of the shamrock, the soil of the free.

Wales at the sound of his angry voice shaketh,
  Scotland shrinks back at the crown on his brow,
But when the proud bosom of Erin's son quaketh,
  Refuse, Holy Mother, thy aid to his vow:
    By the mercy that shieldeth,
      The fallen in strife,
    By the valor that yieldeth,
      The sword but with life,
To sheathe not the steel till the spoiler shall flee
From the land of the shamrock, the soil of the free.

WAR SONG OF FREEDOM.

Charge! while the trumpet yet swells in the blast,
The banners are waving — the war-steeds fly past!
On! for the blade of the foeman is flashing
    As bright as the meteor that falls from the sky!
On! for the bayonet with breastplate is clashing
    As wild as the forest when whirlwinds rush by!
Charge! while the trumpet yet rings in the blast,
The banners are waving, the war-steeds fly past.

The war-steeds are fallen, they sleep in their gore,
The voice of the riders will cheer them no more.
For the Genius of Freedom at midnight descended,
    And whispered her name in the ear of the foe,
And when the charmed sound with the battle-shout
    blended,
    He bowed like the reed or he fled like the roe.
The war-steeds are fallen, they sleep in their gore,
The voice of the riders will cheer them no more.

THE DEAD WARRIOR.

"The morning sun is shining bright upon the battle plain,
And still thou sleep'st. Wake, warrior, wake, and mount thy steed again!
His bristling mane redeemed from gore is floating free and fast
Upon the breeze as it was wont before the battle blast.
Thrice hath the war-peal thundered on since thou hast sunk to rest, —
Did'st thou not hear it in thy dream and grasp thy fallen crest?
And thrice the banner of the foe hath swept in mockery by, —
Did not the gleaming of its stars arrest thy glazing eye?
The charger waits his rider's voice — impatient for the rein;
A foeman speaks, Oh, warrior, wake, and mount thy steed again!"

"Ah, noble foeman, cease thine aid," a weeping mother sung,
While sadly on the sighing winds the mournful music rung.

"Ah, noble foeman, cease thine aid and hush thy
 voice of cheer!
Thou can'st not wake my warrior boy who sleeps
 in silence here.
I 've combed his flowing flaxen hair and from it
 wiped the dew;
Come, gaze upon the lofty brow which in the strife
 ye knew,
And if thy bosom e'er hath burned a warrior's joys
 to know,
Oh! read them on that marble cheek and in a
 mother's woe.
My boy, they said that Fame would twine the
 laurel green for thee;
Alas! alas! but she hath left the cypress sear for
 me."

THE ASSEMBLY.

Hark! 't is the trumpet's call
  Booms o'er the sea!
Crowd for your banners, all,
  Sons of the free!
Send the hoarse battle-yell
  Back to the main!
Arm for the citadel!
  Arm for the plain!

War from his battle-cloud
  Beckons his hand;
Wove is the crimson shroud,
  Drawn be the brand.
Up! from the mount and glen,
  Forest and ford,
Rally! ye free-born men,
  Arm with the sword!

Omens are gathering
  Fast o'er the lea;
Red is the eagle's wing,
  Restless the sea.
When the mast quivereth
  Heed ye the storm,
Arm mid the trumpet's breath,
  Marshal and form!

THE WARRIOR BARD.

Up from his harp the minstrel sprung
   And drew his shining blade ; .
"I cannot sing as once I sung,
   Nor play as once I played.
An omen strange invests my soul,
   And breaks its wonted dream,
I hear far off the war-bolt roll,
   I see the red brand gleam.

While swift amid the dark'ning sky,
   As hoarse the trumpet sings,
There seems an eagle rushing by,
   With blood upon his wings.
It is no dream — no mocking sight —
   It is no mind-wrought spell —
Come from thy sheath, thou *vassal bright*,
   And smooth my war-path well!

Where floats amid the battle storm
   Yon emblem of the free,
There in the foeman's life-blood warm
   I'll trace my name with thee."
He said — and left the peaceful plain
   To seek the hostile shore,
But e'er his harp was tuned again,
   He fell to rise no more.

SONG OF THE DRAGOON.

Our march is like the thunder gust!
   We prostrate where we pass.
And broader is the trail we leave
   Along the tangled grass.
From North to South we range the wood,
   We tread the wilds afar,
We thread the brake, we swim the flood,
   Onward! Huzza, huzza!

Our halt is where the prairie wolf
   Barks at the grizzly bear,
And every robe we lie upon
   The buffalo must spare.
Break not, my boys, the squadron's line,
   Down with the forest spar!
Cut with your swords the tangled vine!
   Onward! Huzza, huzza!

Our steeds are like ourselves, my boys,
   Born for a martial train,
Fearless and strong they prance along.
   And yet they *heed the rein.*
Then let the merry bugle sound,
   We'll follow Freedom's star
For battle, or for hunting-ground, —
   Onward! Huzza, huzza!

THE WAR-DRUM.

The war-drum beats throughout the land
   The red man swore to yield,
A thousand braves have drawn the brand.
   Go arm ye for the field.
And let in words of crimson dye
   Each flag one motto claim, —
We greet no friend but Victory,
   We fear no foe but Shame.

The tawny hunter laughs in scorn,
   And taunts ye to the plain,
"The knife is red — the scalp is torn,
   Ye dare not seek your slain."
And is it thus, ye freemen wed,
   Defenders of the right?
Comrades! arise and *seek* your dead;
   Go arm ye for the fight.

Where is the spirit of the past?
   The Chivalry of yore?
Where are the whirlwinds of the blast,
   The hearts your Father's bore?
Where are they? Comrades, *they are here*,
   Up, rally, one and all,

Rise and avenge the orphan's tear —
Avenge a *Frazer's* fall.*

* *Avenge a Frazer's fall.* Alluding to Major Frazer, a much-esteemed officer of the Third Artillery, who fell at Dade's Massacre, which took place on the road from Tampa Bay to Fort King, Florida, December 28th, 1835.

Several particulars of this disastrous affair were gleaned from the lips of one of the survivors, a soldier by the name of Sprague. The statement, given nearly in his own words, is as follows: —

"We left Tampa Bay for Fort King on Christmas morning. The command consisted of three companies of Artillery, under Major Dade, armed as Infantry, with the exception of a small field-piece, taken along as a precautionary measure in case of an attack, although, owing to our numbers, little danger of an assault was anticipated. For the first two days nothing occurred to excite our apprehensions, but on the third day of the route, as the troops, marching in loose order, were approaching a dense wood which skirted the road, we were suddenly startled by the war-whoop, followed by a severe fire from the Indians, who were concealed behind the trunks of trees, and also among the branches.

"A portion of the guard, which preceded the wagons, together with Major Frazer who was also in advance, was shot down by the first volley, and the remainder retreated to the main body which, as soon as it could be brought up, rallied in front of the baggage train and returned the fire.

"The Indians, in no wise intimidated by the display of our men, then came out from their hiding places and attacked us in force.

"The fight raged for several hours, and, owing to the superior number of the assaulting party, we should probably at that time have been worsted, had it not been for the effective fire from the field-piece, which so disconcerted the enemy that he was forced to retire. After the savages had fled we commenced calling the roll, when it was found that at least one half of the command was either killed or wounded. Major Dade had fallen soon after the death of Major Frazer.

"At this juncture had a retreat been ordered, it is quite possible that the remainder of the command might have reached Tampa

Bay without further molestation, but the few surviving officers would not listen to the proposition; so we commenced fortifying ourselves within a hollow square constructed of logs and such quantities of brush-wood as could be made available for that purpose.

"We had scarcely arranged our defenses when the Indians again appeared — this time accompanied by a large body of negroes — and completely surrounded us.

"Notwithstanding the desperate resistance of the troops, the enemy gained the stockade, climbed over the breastworks, and commenced an indiscriminate slaughter of every one within the inclosure.

"Those disabled by wounds, as well as those who continued to make a show of resistance, were inhumanly butchered, the negroes outvieing the Indians in their deeds of atrocity. Assistant Surgeon Gatlin, Lieutenants Mudge and Basinger were the last murdered.

"When the savages approached Lieutenant Basinger, where he lay wounded, he raised himself on his elbow and plead for life piteously, but was answered with imprecations by one of the negroes, who buried his hatchet in his brains.

"While the work of slaughter was progressing, although severely wounded myself, I retained sufficient composure to remain perfectly quiet. The enemy, no doubt imagining that I was dead, passed over without molesting me. Two of my comrades made use of a similar artifice, and in this manner like myself succeeded in saving their lives. Soon after the savages had departed, my two friends joined me, and creeping cautiously over the bodies of the slain, we managed to gain a neighboring swamp, where we remained nearly waist-deep in water throughout the night. The next morning, perceiving no signs of the Indians, we crept out and proceeded cautiously on our journey back to Tampa Bay.

"The coldness of the water in the swamp had staunched the bleeding of our wounds, so that we were enabled to travel along slowly — gathering palmetto-roots and berries for food along the road, until we again reached the Bay, bringing with us the first and last intelligence ever received from the command after its departure from that station."

Such is a brief outline of some of the incidents connected with this unfortunate expedition, as related by one of the sufferers who, after the massacre, was assigned to the same company which the writer of this notice commanded.

It may not be uninteresting to add that a monument commemorative of the tragic event, whereon are engraved the names of the fallen officers, has been recently erected on the classic grounds appertaining to the Military Academy at West Point.

THE ARMY IN THE FIELD.

I never see a shadowy plume
    Upon a soldier's crest,
But I think of you, my gallant braves,
    Amid the far Southwest.
I never hear the fife's shrill notes
    Amid the city's hum,
But I see your serried columns form
    Where rolls the roaring drum.

A lengthened trail ye tread, my braves,
    And difficult its sign,
Through hummock and through everglade,
    By marsh and tangled vine.
Your homestead is the wilderness,
    Your canopy the sky,
And the music which ye love the most
    Lives in the battle-cry.

They little know, who lightly dwell
    Upon the griefs ye bear,
The task and toil — oh, weary ones —
    Which ye are doomed to share.
'T is yours to quench the feudal fire,
    The elements prolong;

To hunt the footsteps of the fierce,
   To wrestle with the strong;

To scorch beneath the vernal sun
   Amid the hurried rout;
To scare the vulture from his feast
   Where the foremost steed gave out;
To seek in vain for gushing spring
   Upon a sterile waste;
To roam amid the mazy wood,
   With the homeward path effaced.

'T is yours to scorn what fear deride,
   Attempt where all may fail,
To stem the raging of the tide,
   The rushing of the gale;
And when your hearts of lava rock
   Heave like the mountain warm,
'T is yours to roll unto the shock,
   Like the torrent and the storm.

And oh! 't is yours, at midnight hour,
   Upon the guarded plain,
To dream of smiles far, far away,
   Ye ne'er may see again;
To vanquish hope, to purchase fame
   With blood of foe unseen;
Then find a grave without a name
   Beneath the hummock green.

    FORT KING, *Florida.*

THE TRUMPET.

What charm, O Trumpet, sways thy breath,
   That man so doats on thee,
Fierce tempter to the field of death,
   Yet arbiter of glee?
And the Trumpet answered on the blast,
   With its wild and wildering tone, —
"I bind the present and the past,
   With a magic all my own.

"There's a charm that lives for the vine-clad
   bower,
   And one for the sparkling wine,
And one for the lute, of a queenly power,
   But a stronger spell is mine.
I speak to the ear of restless Love,
   And his burning eyes grow dim,
As he turns from his bride in the homestead
   grove,
   Where impatient she waits for him.

"The battle stirreth at my word
   Its elements of fear;
Leaps from its sheath the restless sword,
   Flashes the potent spear.

The war-drum rolls a wilder call,
   And the bristling columns form;
Red streams the death-flag from the wall,
   Rattles the leaden storm.

" My voice is o'er the sleeping seas,
   And on the surging shore,
I sing upon the rustling breeze,
   And I speak where tempests roar.
The squadron bark knows not her own,
   Till she hears my signal blast,
While the wrecker watcheth for my tone,
   As he bows by the bending mast.

" Well did they heed my daring call
   In the city of the plain,*
When rushed the foemen from the wall
   As it crumbled o'er the slain.
And I have a tone I yet must wind
   For the ear of earthful lust,
When I tear apart the chains which bind
   The sleeper to the dust."

          * Jericho.

LINES ON A DECEASED COMRADE.

WRITTEN AT WEST POINT ACADEMY.

STILL as the dreamless dead
   Was the solemn house of prayer,
Save when the low command was said,
Or the distant sound of measured tread,
   Broke on the silence there.

They come, I see them now,
   With their plumes of sable dye;
There is manhood's pride on boyhood's brow,
And the bearing proud of those who bow
   To naught but the shrine on high.

Why have ye gathered here,
   Ye of the youthful band?
Why do ye brush the starting tear,
And with arms reversed beside yon bier,
   Why do ye speechless stand?

I heard a sullen sigh,
   And I heard a hollow groan,
And a strain of music wild and high,
Like the voice of a spirit wailing nigh,
   Amid the winds' deep moan.

Aye! roll the muffled drum,
   And chant the funeral air!
For the brow is cold and the lips are dumb
Of him with whom ye were wont to come
   To the holy place of prayer.

How calm and still he lies,
   In his sleep devoid of pain!
Like a weary child he hath closed his eyes,
And sank to rest. But when will he rise?
   When will he wake again?

Not when to-morrow's dawn
   Is told by the cannon's roar,
Not when the bugle winds at morn:
Like a wandering bird his spirit is borne,
   To return to its home no more.

THE DREAM OF BATTLE.

"Wake, wake! 'tis morn, for the battle-horn
   Was to sound at break of day,
And loud and clear its notes I hear;
   Wake, warrior, and away!
Thy falchion bright thou must dim, brave knight,
   With many a blood-red stain,
Ere the rising sun which ye gaze upon
   Shall gild the west again.
And the flying feet of thy charger fleet
   Must bound o'er many a foe,
When rolling nigh from yonder sky,
   The battle-cloud sweeps low.
But the name of a maid is inscribed on thy blade,
   And resistless its flash will be,
And her sunny-bright hair thy heart doth wear,
   From danger a charm to free.
Then awake, 'tis morn,' for the battle-horn
   Was to sound at break of day,
And loud and clear its notes I hear;
   Up! warrior, and away."

The minstrel paused, but still her eye
Was fixed upon the sunset sky,
Gazing as if her spirit drew
An inspiration from its hue;

As if communion she could share
With the etherial essence there.
But when the sun with burning crest
Had sunk beneath the molten west,
And pensive Night drew o'er the plain
Her curtained veil of shadowy stain,
As if partaking of its hue,
The minstrel's measure saddened too.

"Why, maiden fair, why roaming there,
  Alone on the battle-heath?
Why dost thou stray where the fallen lay
  Sleeping the sleep of death?
Oh, wild and lone is the deep winds' moan,
  And the waning moon shines drear!
What warrior pale in his gory mail
  Resteth in silence here?
Go, weeping maid, the cypress braid,
  It must be thy bridal wreath,
For the steed at thy feet was the steed so fleet,
  And the rider was crushed beneath.
When the war-blast came he breathed thy name,
  And I saw the foeman flee,
And I saw the dart as it pierced his heart,
  While he shouted, 'Victory!'
Again at morn the battle-horn,
  May sound the break of day,
But its voice of cheer he will never hear;
  Weep, maiden, and away!"

SONG OF THE WRECKER.

When swiftly glides the fleecy wrack
   Athwart the troubled sky,
'T is ours to plow the foamy track
   Of billows heaving by;
And as we hear o'er waves afar
   The tempest's rushing wing,
Deep rolling on his clouded car,
   We hail the Thunder-king.

In bondage calm the morning haze
   May hold the idle deep;
We care not where the dolphin plays,
   Nor where the mermaids sleep.
But when the gathering tempest forms,
   And wheeling sea-birds sing,
High lifted to the shrine of storms,
   We hail the Thunder-king.

The voice on shore may swell its bowers
   With music rich and bland;
We answer not with notes of ours,
   The melodies of land.

But when the god of ocean wakes
   His lyre, of lordly string,
While hoarse the surging billow breaks,
   We hail the Thunder-king.

Then should some bark bewildered glide
   Across our stormy track,
Where once beguiled the whirling tide
   Gives not its victim back,
Each stranger knows what craft are we,
   And waits the aid we bring,
As louder than the lashing sea
   We hail the Thunder-king.

THE DYING VOLUNTEER.

HERE, comrades, rest me here,
   Beside the grassy road ;
Let yon soft couch, where Autumn sear
Hath cast her robes from year to year,
   Receive your weary load.

Leave me where breezes play
   Mid palm-trees waving high,
And flowers exert such pleasing sway,
That Death himself aside might stray,
   Forgetting where I lie !

Counsel yon leaping stream
   To strike its thunder strain ;
And let awhile its billowy gleam
Invest my sight — that I may dream
   The battle wakes again ;

That blazing banners fly
   Where steeds impatient stand,
And as I breathe my latest sigh,
Of dying, as I hoped to die,
   With the falchion in my hand.

For this I left my home —
  But the fevered dream is past —
No more upon my ear will come
The war-beat of the gathering drum,
  Nor the trumpet's rousing blast.

The star hath set in night,
  Which once so fair did shine.
Wresting, forever, from my sight
Column deep serried for the fight,
  And square and wheeling line.

Upon the battle-bed,
  While rang the banner cry,
Gazing upon the eagle dread,
With his shadowy wings to the fight outspread,
  It was my prayer to die;

Not thus unwept, alone,
  To yield my failing breath,
Where the hot day-breeze hath a tone
Accordant with the fevered groan
  Of melancholy death.

Yet not in vain shall flee
  My life's departing ray!
Comrades, go tell them who, like me,
Have pined to sail on Glory's sea,
  How little wise are they.

And mention, as ye came
  Along the wandering wave,
How on a spot without a name,
Far hidden from the shrine of Fame,
  Ye paused beside my grave.

TAMPA BAY, *Florida.*

LANDING OF THE FLORIDA REGULARS AT TAMPA BAY,

OCTOBER, 1837.

Strike up the rattling drum!
   Shake out the guidon free!
Hurra! with succoring bands we come
   Across the bounding sea.

We near the hostile shore,
   Flourish the bugles' blast!
Our weary voyage at length is o'er,
   Hurra! we land at last.

Hurra — hurra — hurra!
   For yonder tented plain!
In grasp of peace with hands of war,
   We greet our friends again.

Stand, comrades, on your lives!
   Fill twice the wine-cup round!
Pledge once your homes and once your wives,
   Then dash it to the ground.

Perchance that cup may pass,
   Some later hour again,

And ye may drink *who fill that glass*,
   The memory of the slain.

Raise up the banner high
   As the Grecian held his targe!
If die we must like men we die,
   Sound! forward to the charge.

March on with measured tread!
   'T is Glory leads and Fame —
Our hunter hands the toils have spread,
   The war-hounds scent the game.

Wait for the word — step light!
   Let not a breath respire!
Aim to the left — the right —
   Aim to the centre — fire!

Hurra — hurra — hurra!
   I love the stormy din,
As fierce and fast, like waves afar,
   The battle roareth in.

The music of the strife —
   The war-bolt flashing by —
The forfeit death — the guerdon life —
   Hurra for victory!

THE WASTE WORN.

Weary and weak and pale,
   He sank on the lengthened route;
And they paused awhile in the lowly vale,
   Where his fevered frame gave out.

No gentle hand strewed flowers
   Along his rude-made bier,
The death-stained leaves from the oak's old bowers,
   They scattered with pike and spear.

Eyes gazed but grew not dim
   Beside his pulseless clay.
Though grief had treasured depths for him
   In a fount — oh, far away —

Deep buried in the breast
   Of one, from crowds apart,
Watching with brow of troubled rest
   For the partner of her heart.

When, when will he return?
   Fond thoughts his course may track,
Heart throb and bosom burn —
   But when will he come back?

When Spring's first flowers shall fall,
   Autumn's last leaf is sear,
Will she meet his smile? will she hear his call?
   Oh, ask of the guarded bier.

Beneath a southern sky,
   Without a hymn or prayer,
They made a grave mid the palm-trees high,
   And alone they laid him there.

No, no! — 't was not alone —
   For the drum gave out its roll,
And the woods chimed deep in an undertone,
   A knell for the loosened soul;

And the twilight drew around,
   With its pale and sickly smile,
And the stream discoursed in its rushing sound,
   And the mock-bird sang the while.

Sweet bird of memory dear,
   Thy melody is vain,
He heareth not, — he cannot hear, —
   When will he wake again?

BOYHOOD.

I never see the laughing eyes
    Of joyous boys at play,
But memories fond within me rise,
    Of childhood's happy day.
To sport upon the festive ground
    Seemed all I had to do,
And when my comrades laughed around,
    My heart was happy too.

I seldom cared for dust and noise,
    Or wore a troubled brow,
But thought myself with marble toys
    Oh, richer far than now.
I never pined for foreign land,
    Nor sighed for distant sea,
The top which turned beneath my hand
    Had charms enough for me.

But now upon my troubled soul
    Come visions dark and deep,
My thoughts are where the billows roll,
    And where the whirlwinds sweep.
I love to see the bending mast
    Bow down before the storm,

And hear amid the rushing blast,
  The *wing* without a form.

I wander o'er the plain of death,
  As through a lady's bower,
Deep watching for the battle breath,
  As for a thought of power.
Alas! the lesson manhood brings,
  And little understood —
To leave the lore of gentle things,
  For toil by field and flood.

Flow on, calm blood of childhood, flow!
  Speed not your current thin!
Nor let the conscious bosom know
  The fires which burn within.
Too soon will come the moment when
  Each pulse anew will start,
And thou, the purple tide of men,
  Must battle with the heart.

THE TWO VOICES.

Two voices swelled athwart the lea,
   I listened while they sang;
One, soft as lute upon the sea;
   One, like the trumpet's clang.

FIRST VOICE.

Daughter, rest: no cloud of sorrow
   Dews thy brow with tears of stain,
Sleep to-night — the dawning morrow
   Soon will smile for thee again;
Starlight sleeps upon the water,
   Sunlight slumbers in the west,
Close thine eyelids, gentle daughter,
   Nature's voices whisper " Rest."

Daughter, rest; I smooth thy pillow,
   Lay thy head upon it, sweet;
Here doth never dash the billow;
   Here the drum may never beat.
Sight of war will ne'er come o'er thee,
   Sound of strife affright thy breast;
But thy father's lip before thee,
   In thy dream shall murmer " Rest."

Daughter, rest; no thorn shall wound thee,
   'Mid thy dream of roses wild,
Mother's arm is clasped around thee,
   Mother rocks her cradled child.
Sleep! the weary herd is folded,
   Drowsy birds have sought their nest,
Hush! the song which father molded,
   Dies in silence. Daughter, Rest!

Two voices swelled athwart the lea,
   I listened while they sang :
One, soft as lute upon the sea ;
   One, like the trumpet's clang.

SECOND VOICE.

Forward! mid the battles' hum
   Roughly rolls the daring drum !
Victory, with hurried breath,
   Calls ye from her mouths of death !
War, with hand of crimson stain,
   Warns ye to the front again !
Onward! ere the field is won,—
   Forward! ere the fight is done.

Forward! raise your banner high!
   Toss its spangles to the sky!
Let its eagle, reeking red,
   Float above the foeman's head!
Let its stripes of red and white
   Blind again his dazzled sight!

Onward! ere the field is won,—
  Forward! ere the fight is done.

Forward! to the front again!
  Lash the steed and loose the rein!
Spur amid the rattling peal!
  Charge amid the storm of steel!
O'er the stream and from the glen,
  Cowards watch the strife of men; *
Onward! ere the field is won,—
  Forward! ere the fight is done!

---

* Probably alluding to a certain battle on the banks of the Withlacoochie, Florida, where it was said certain troops could not be brought into action.

THE SOLDIER'S VISION.

From his bed on the field overshadowed by night,
    Where the living unconscious lay mixed with the slain,
'T was thus that a soldier, forgetting the fight,
    Soft murmured in dreams from the slumber-girt plain: —

'T is the haunt of the savage! from yonder lone creek
    He gazes unnoticed on pennon and spear;
'T is the dew-drops of midnight which gleam on the cheek,
    And the bay of the blood-hound which startles the ear.

The steed is ungirt and the rider at rest,
    Deep lulled by the tongues of the many-toned gales,
While Memory's fond watchwords steal over his breast,
    Like the voice of a friend when the challenger hails.

But Sleep to this bosom brings not the relief
    He is wont to bestow where his poppies are spread;

O'er my couch of repose bends the cypress of grief,
   And my heart's dearest rose-buds lie scattered and dead.

Those glass-works of Fancy — the day-dreams of youth,
   Like the mists of the morning have melted away,
While Hope, like a mock sun, all bright with untruth,
   Conceals mid the tempest her storm-fostered ray.

They told me how Honor doled gifts from the sky,
   And I came to the field where his guerdons are won,
But Fame, like a falcon, flew wary and high,
   And Glory played false, as the battle swept on.

Next Fortune, on pinions impatient to roam,
   Sang softly the charms of her gold-yielding land,
But my vision of wealth proved a plaything of foam,
   And the air-bubble burst ere it sailed from my hand.

Then Love gently came to my slumber-sealed eyes,
   And I prayed for the meed which the warm-hearted share,
But the god, when invoked, threw aside his disguise,
   And the herald of Joy proved a phantom of care.

Soft hope of my bosom! bright pledge of my vow!
   What climate invests thee — surrounds thee what shore?
I see not the light of thy love-beaming brow,
   And I catch the low sound of thy murmurs no more.

The fall of thy footstep what chamber may claim,
   Thou dove borne astray on the wings of the blast?
E'en the lute, so vibrating to murmur thy name,
   Grows sad, at the sound, as a voice from the past.

Then the dreamer awoke from his vision of care,
   And he saw but the moon shining low in the west,
While the wing of the night-wind played loose in his hair,
   And the palm-leaf's deep shadow lay hushed on his breast.

In the Field, *Florida*, 1838.

THE SOLDIER'S REQUIEM.*

    A SWORD unclaimed and a crest!
Did ye not hear that muffled knell
Mid the measured pause of a trumpet's swell?
    They bear him to his rest.

    Dreary and wild and deep!
Why soften the voice of your clarion clear?
Why smother the roll at the guarded bier?
    His is a dreamless sleep.

    Give to your bugles breath!
Ye will rouse him not from his bannered shroud!
Ye will wrest him not from his victor proud!
    A conqueror strong is Death.

    Onward and on, but slow!
Steady and slow, it is weight ye hold —
Precious it lies 'neath the flag's deep fold —
    Weight that ye little know.

    There was a spirit nurst!
There was a heart which beat for fame,

---

* Written upon the death of Lieutenant JOSEPH RITNER, son of Governor Ritner of Pennsylvania.

A hand which struck for a soldier's name ;
  On, with the manly dust!

Comrade! thine eye is dim ;
No more will its drooping lid be raised ;
Alas! that the lute thou oft hast praised
  Should chant thy requiem hymn!

Thy voice will sound no more,
As in cadenced thunder once it fell,
When the soldier's shout and the Indian's yell
  Thrilled the Wisconsin shore.

No more the jest will stray,
Nor the smile of glee nor the joyous song
From thy lip, as the heavy route wears long
  On the soldier's weary way.

Comrade, thy task is done!
Pennon and plume beside thee meet ;
They move to the roll of the last retreat
  Which marks thy setting sun.

Give to your bugles breath!
Ye can wake him not from his bannered shroud!
Ye can wrest him not from his victor proud!
  A conqueror strong is Death.

COME, LET US DIE LIKE MEN.

Roll out the banner on the air,
    And draw your swords of flame.
The gathering squadrons fast prepare
    To take the field of fame!
In serried ranks, your columns dun
    Close up along the glen;
If we must die ere set of sun,
    Come, let us die like men.

We seek the foe from night till morn,
    A foe we do not see.
Go, roll the drum and wind the horn,
    And tell him here are we.
In idle strength we wait the prey
    That lurks by marsh and fen;
But should he strike our lines to-day,
    Come, let us die like men.

'T is not to right a kinsman's wrongs,
    With bristling arms we come.
Our sisters sing their household songs
    Far in a peaceful home.
We battle for a stranger's hall,
    The savage in his den,

If in such struggle we must fall,
  Come, let us die like men.

Remember, boys, that Mercy's dower
  Is life to him who yields,
Remember that the hand of power
  Is strongest when it shields :
Keep honor, like your sabres, bright,
  Shame coward fear — and then
If we *must* perish in the fight —
  Oh, we will die like men!

FORT MONIAC, *Florida,*
  Dec. 16*th*, 1838.

THE WIND SPIRIT.

SHEATHED was the sabre's restless gleam,
   And the trump had ceased to play,
As the day-star shed its last red beam
   On the couch where a soldier lay:
Soft citrons sighed on the Southern air,
   But what was their breath to him?
Toil drooping weighed on his brow of care,
   And his drowsy eyes grew dim.

"Oh, let me sleep one little hour,
   I'm weary of the tented ground!
The breezes kiss the nodding flower,
   And softly steals the riplet's sound;
The mock-birds sing mid rustling trees,
   With lazy tread the insects creep,
While drowsily the hum of bees
   Subdues the field. Ah, let me sleep!

"Oh, let me sleep, once more to fly
   Where first in early years I sung!
I cannot brook this Southern sky,
   I cannot love the Southrons' tongue;
But bear me to my native isle,
   Which wild the lashing billows sweep, —

There once for me were lips of smile, —
   Where dwell they now? Ah! let me sleep!

"Oh, let me sleep; for in the brief
   Bright hour of trance which dreams bestow,
I hear again the rustling leaf
   That whirls around my home of snow;
I see the pine of mountain birth,
   Still green above the hoary steep,
And at the household's blazing hearth
   I breathe a name, — Ah! let me sleep."

And he slept — he slept — and the North wind came
   From his home in a Northern land,
Deep whispering many a cherished name,
   O'er the brow which its pinions fanned;
And the dreamer hailed the well-known sound,
   As the voice of an absent friend,
And he questioned the breeze, as it whirled around,
   Of the forms it had left behind.

"Wind of the North! whose pinions high
   Against my forehead play,
What seek'st thou mid a Southern sky,
   And the battle's red array?
Yet welcome from thy snow-wreathed hill,
   To a sultry clime like ours,

Come, mingle a gust, thou minion chill,
　　With the breath of the palm-leaf bowers.

"Full well I knew thy car was near,
　　Ere rolled its thunder loud,
For I saw thy frost-white charioteer
　　Careering o'er the cloud.
Come gently to my fevered brow,
　　With genial freshness come;
And tell me, Wind, but whisper low,
　　When did'st thou pass my home?"

"Thy home? — since morn I swept beside
　　The arch of its portal high,
Where I saw a bride with a brow of pride,
　　And a tear was in her eye."
"And did ye not catch that truant tear
　　Ere it fell at the festive board?"
"I did — and she bade me drop it *here* —
　　On the heart of her absent lord."

"What saw'st thou next?" — "A child at play
　　I saw by the hearth of glee."
"And did ye not pause upon the way,
　　To kiss its brow for me?"
"I lingered an hour, well pleased the while,
　　Lifting her tresses bright,
And wasting my breath on her lips of smile —
　　Hence I am late to-night."

"Wind of the North, thy wings unfold!
　　Back to my home return,
And tell her that thy kiss is cold,
　　But there are lips which burn, —
Whose every breath along her cheek
　　Such gentle tales would tell
As whispering fancy loves to speak; —
　　Wind of the North, farewell!"

THE GATHERING.

Sound ye the tocsin from Maine to Missouri,
   Light the red signals and toll the alarm!
Wake the war-hounds with the lash of the Fury,
   Blood is the cry, and the watchword is Arm!
        Burst ye asunder
        The portals of thunder,
Which masked the stern god in his temple* so long,
   And on your three-deckers store spars for a jury,
The best mast may fall, though the cedar be strong.

You is the steed all arrayed for the battle.
   See how he paweth and pants for the plain!
'T is the clash of the sabre — he knoweth its rattle —
   Spring to the saddle and yield him the rein!
        Bold as your manners,
        Flourish your banners,
   Strike for the star of the eagle and shield!
For woman 't is sighs — and for children 't is prattle,
   For *men* 't is the trumpet which sounds to the field.

---

* Alluding to the Temple of Janus which was closed in times of peace, but kept open during the period of war.

Passion-bound minstrel, abandon your numbers,
  Snap the soft lute-string or cut it with steel!
Herdsmen and husbandmen, wake from your slumbers!
'T is the voice of the tempest, the forest will reel —
      Country and city,
      Honest and witty,
Gather in — gather round — hark to the laws!
The incense burns not for the cloud which encumbers,
  Arm! arm for the people, and strike for the cause!

The victim is slain and the entrails are heaving *
  Portentous with omens 't is fearful to sing,
While the bird of the storm through the red tempest cleaving
  Floats fast to the South on his thunder-nerved wing.
      Landsmen and seamen,
      Bondmen and freemen,
Rally up — rally on — look to the sign!
Dark is the spell which the augurs are weaving;
  Stand to your colors and crowd to the line.

February, 1861.

---

* The Romans are said to have derived their auguries by observing the palpitation of the entrails of beasts slain at the sacrificial altars of their priests.

SONG OF THE YOUNG SCOUT.

I LOVE to wear my weapon bright,
   But not alone for show;
Though at my side 't is seeming light,
   'T is heavy in the blow;
They watch me twine in dalliance oft
   Its knot of silk and gold;
And wonder how a hand so soft
   Should gripe a thing so cold.

I roam along the hostile shore,
   Where lurks the tawny clan,
I hear the rifle's stirring roar,
   And I lead my foremost man.
My path is o'er the blood-red trail,
   Which flying feet have past,
Rattles around the leaden hail,
   Echoes the trumpet's blast.

'T is mine the torrent's bed to wade,
   Urged by the "long alarm,"
And through the hummock's friendless shade
   To charge the lifted arm.
I'm on my steed — I know his spring
   Along the grassy plain;

Give way — he hears the clarion ring,
  And chafeth 'neath the rein.

Oh, what to me your chidings loud,
  Or prayers of pleading warm?
I wrestle with the tempest cloud,
  I worship — with the storm.
And what the voice that chants at home
  Its drowsy roundelay? —
Go, sing unto the wild sea's foam,
  And bid the billows stay.

For me the music of the wind,
  That shakes the rocking trees,
All gentler strains I leave behind;
  My mistress is the breeze!
Rouse up, my merry men, and share
  My fortune, lost or won!
The larum rolls along the air, —
  On! to the conflict, on!

THE YOUNG WARRIOR.

Fast fell a sighing sister's tears upon a brother's brow,
As stole upon the moaning winds a voice of murmurs low:
"What wilt thou, brother, with thy sword and with thy trappings gay?
And canst thou leave us, Oh! beloved, far more than words can say?
What secret charm can urge thee forth to meet the savage foe?
I grieve for thee, my brother; alas! that thou shouldst go!
I weep, I cling unto thy neck, and wilt thou not remain?
Do lips of prayer and eyes of love still plead and gush in vain?
Then forth! and take with thee my heart, 't will guard thee in the fight,
For woman in her love is strong as a warrior in his might."

A father's voice rose solemnly in cadence grave but mild,
As tremulous his aged form came tottering to his child:

"I ne'er like thee have doated on the glories of
    the field,
Nor did I tell thee, boy, to choose the weapon thou
    dost wield;
'T is thine the chances of the die, the fortune lost
    or won,
And yet I bless thee in my grief — I bless thee,
    Oh! my son.
Would that my trembling form for thee the task
    and toil might bear,
That I might suffer for my child, the cherished
    of my prayer.
May He who smiles amid the storm rebuke the
    bolts of harm,
My dearest and my latest born, I yield thee to His
    arm."

Then heavily, came heavily, like ocean's wintry
    moan,
Amid the pausing of her sobs, a mother's broken
    tone:
"I press thee in these aged arms, my dearest and
    my last —
And wilt thou leave our peaceful home for the
    torrent and the blast?
I knew, my child, the trump and drum were all
    thy early dream,
But canst thou hear them in thy sleep amidst the
    purple stream?
I knew thy gaze was earnest when a banner floated
    by,

But can the gleaming of its stars arrest the clos-
    ing eye?
My son, my son, to lose thee thus a mother may
    not bear!
And shall I kiss no more thy brow, nor part thy
    shining hair;
Nor gaze in silence on thy face, nor linger on thy
    word?
Oh! by a mother's tongueless grief, yield up the
    tearless sword!"

As melts the bugle's dying note along the tented
    plain,
Then deeply chimed that warrior's voice in a tone
    of understrain:
"The varied changes of the field mine is the lot to
    know;
I've stood where swords were flashing bright and
    banners waving low,
And I have felt while hoarsely rang the trumpet
    voice of Fame,
That Conquest was a weary word and Glory but a
    name;
And yet, and yet, Oh! most beloved, when duty
    calls away,
To battle for my country's right, I may not, must
    not stay!
Though dreadful be the fountain red where drinks
    the thirsty sword,
Oh! judge ye not the mailèd might of Gideon and
    the Lord."

SONGS OF THE BOWER.

"Oh, God! that you may never know
How wild a kiss she gave to me!" — *Anon.*

THE DREAMING BOY.

My mother called me oft her dreaming boy,
   Even from my youth's spring-time — for I took
But little pleasure in the task or toy;
   And if my eyes at times were on my book,
My thoughts were wandering elsewhere. 'T was my
     joy
   To steal alone to some sequestered brook;
And I would leave my playmates in their glee,
To watch the sun go down upon the sea.

Such was a quaint caprice, but harmless, sure,
   Yet Envy brooked it not, and she would say,
(Pointing her fingers with a look demure,)
   "There goes the misanthrope who shuns the play
Of his companions." And I did endure
   It all — save once, when, on a festal day
An urchin called me " Coward." Face to face
We met, — Ah! 't was a long unkind embrace.

Mine was a gentle nature — yet a look
   Reproachful, or a word, I could not bear,

And if they ever crossed me with rebuke,
  I gnashed my teeth, and stormed, and tore my
      hair;
Or hiding in some dark sequestered nook,
  Vexatious wept myself to slumber there.
Yet there was *one* whose voice of undertone
Could soothe my anger with a look alone.

I prized her much; for she would often turn
  To paint the "stars" upon my new-made kite,
And clap her hands, and skip for joy to learn
  The story gay of its successful flight.
My "*puzzle*" too — when I could not discern
  What piece "*came next,*" *she* always told me
      right;
And on the rocks, beside the sounding sea,
She'd sit, and string my shells and sing to me.

I knew her guileless, simply — that she *sung*.
  (Music, I'm sure, could never wed with Wrong;
Oh! I would list to siren Falsehood's tongue,
  If she but breathed her perjured tale in song.)
Sometimes for me, also, her lute she strung,
  And as her fingers swept the chords along,
If o'er my brow there chanced a cloud of pain,
'T would melt away beneath the magic strain.

Did she but laugh, I know not how or why,
  My ready lip prolonged the joyous trill,

And if her bosom chanced to heave the sigh,
  My own grew sad, swelling responsive still.
When she was near, more bright the sunset sky,
  And softer seemed the rippling of the rill;
In every rose her fingers wandered o'er,
I found some beauty ne'er discerned before.

Again, and yet again, — and a deep dream
  Comes o'er me with the thoughts of days gone by!
And a dim mist rises from Time's dark stream
  And gathers round my brow — oh, heavily!
And through the shadowy vista forms there seem
  Of memory's past creation, and mine eye
Rests, like a dreamer's, on a shape of air:
The ideal of my numbers — *she is there.*

Clear and more clear my sight that mould defines
  Shaped by the wing of symmetry. Her hair
Floats o'er her marble forehead, which reclines
  Upon a Parian arm, — a model rare,
Meet for a master's study, and the lines
  Of more than mortal beauty, — all are there,
Breaking upon my vision from afar,
As through a fleecy cloud the midnight star.

Oh, thou bright being of my wayward song,
  Whose form, like a mysterious presence, slow,
Unshadowed o'er my fancy steals along,
  As o'er the mist at eve a sunset bow,

Leaning upon my hand, with effort strong,
  I gaze upon thy image. Long ago,
Bella! since last we met, — and with a start
I breathe thy name as of past time a part.

Thine oft-heard tone comes o'er me, yet, methinks,
  'T is like the voice of ages in mine ear,
And my bowed spirit chastens as it drinks
  The waters of remembrance with a tear;
And this frail hand at its own easel shrinks,
  Like a discouraged painter's. Oh! the bier
Weareth a robe of gladness, to the pall
Drawn round the soul at wakened memory's call.

Oft we were wont, when first the sunbeams smiled,
  Scattering the pathway with bright gems of dew,
Locked hand in hand, to tread the meadows wild,
  And pluck the hawthorn or the harebell blue;
Or climb the hay-mound when the air was mild,
  And laughing watch the bubbles which we blew,
Or seek the bank, pleased with the streamlet's purl,
Where with the birds she sang, that sinless girl.

And we were wont, when closed the sultry day,
  And the cool breeze reviving freshness bore,
To wander forth along the moon-lit bay,
  And count its ripples as they kissed the shore.
Thrice had I seen her throned the queen of May,
  And thrice the crown *these* fingers wove she wore.
Oh! happy time, how passed the laughing hours
When weaving for *her* brow that crown of flowers.

We've stood together when the lonely lea
' Was hushed around like desolation's fane,
Save when the spirits of the gurgling sea
 Breathed from their caves the murmurs of the main ;
When the faint *South*, weary with flower and tree,
 With folded pinions slept upon its plain ;
And the pale moon looked down upon its crest,
A guardian angel o'er a loved one's rest.

We've stood together when the storm-king bade
 His *own* " go forth " — and heard their answering roar ;
When the wild sea-mews wheeled, with fear dismayed,
 And screamed, and flapped their wings and sought the shore ;
When the thick mist, anon in flames arrayed —
 A horrid beacon — hung the billows o'er ;
All breathless then and pale we've stood to mark
The moving mount where hung the helmless bark.

One breezy night, when shone heaven's silver crown
 Pure as the lustre of an angel's face,
And the far-distant skies seemed bending down
 To clasp the waters in their wide embrace,
On a high beetling crag of rugged frown
 We stood together, far above its base.
'T was a wild rock lashed by the billowy whirl ;
And o'er the brink she gazed, — that fearless girl.

By the crag's verge, bending she stood alone,
  For she had bid me for a moment go
And seek among the cliffs to find a stone,
  That she might plunge it in the gulf below.
'T was but a moment, sure, that I was gone,
  And I had turned to bring one fit to throw,
When a shriek burst above the raving swell, —
"My brain, my brain! *Edgar, save Isabel!*"

Her Edgar heard it, — that wild, frenzied call!
  And a cold, nameless chill his heart came o'er;
The sea-mew heard it from his cloud-capped wall,
  And with a scream accordant fled the shore:
The *storm fiend* heard it in his coral hall,
  And shook his crest and answered with a roar;
And *Echo* heard, and on the mingled swell
Of wind and wave came back, "*Save Isabel!*"

With a quick bound I sprang, wild with dismay,
  But gained the verge too late. — far downward, oh!
On her white dress I saw the moonbeams play,
  Through her loosed hair *glittered the stars below:*
Upon the deep a Parian corse she lay,
  Save one dark spot upon her brow of snow;
Her head drooped down upon a frost-white pillow,
Then sunk, for aye, beneath the heaving billow.

Sky, placid sky, how could'st thou shine the same,
  Mocking my desolation with thy light?

Where were thy red avengers that they came
  Not at my bidding, in that hour of blight?
Earth! where *thy* mercy that thou did'st not claim
  Thy worm and hide him in thy dens of night?
Remorseless deep! why ebbed thy murderous swell?
It had no grave for me — with *Isabel*.

With mad'ning clasp I pressed my burning brain,
  And cast my eyes to heaven! Oh, God! *'t was
    fair;*
No foul eclipse — no cloud of blood-red stain —
  No star came staggering pathless down the air —
But tranquil all and pure — sky, sea and plain —
  Oh! bright and beautiful — and *she was there!*
My every sense — my soul — my all below,
My only light in this dim world of woe.

I threw my form my mother earth beside,
  But on her kindred bosom shed no tear;
My eyes refused to weep, — it was denied
  To soothe my anguish with grief's solace dear;
I did not pray, nor groan, nor rave, nor chide;
  I had no human hope, no earthly fear,
But like the doomed when life's last woof is spun,
Heedless of bloom or blight, or cloud or sun.

I cannot tell how long supine I lay
  Upon the spot where first I listless fell, —
An hour perhaps, perhaps till dawn of day,
  Or the next noon or night, — I cannot tell.

Tides may have ebbed and flowed and the damp
    spray
  Of waves dashed o'er me, — like their sounding
    knell,
The hours passed by, — one long unceasing chime,
One *twilight perpetuity* of time.

At length I recked me of a sound which broke
  The dull monotonous roaring in my ear;
A something like a voice, — methought it spoke
  Pausing and low, as if the dead were near;
And then, methought, I heard a raven croak,
  And moving wheels groan heavily — like a bier;
While my bowed form was lifted up and lain
Upon — I know not what, — 't was dark again.

When next the star of reason lit my soul,
  Upon a couch I lay, and through the fold
Of crimson curtains chastened sunbeams stole,
  Bright'ning my pillow with their rays of gold;
While at a span's brief distance stood a bowl
    Fraught with some soothing draught; strange fits
    of cold
Thrilled through my limbs — methought could I
    obtain
That cup, 't would bring reviving warmth again.

I tried to raise my hand, with effort strong,
  When, oh, despair! it recked not of my will;
I strove to speak — the accents died along

A passage closed to utterance — all was still.
Then beings strange came in, a motley throng,
   And I did pray them not to do me ill,
And showed my pillow where the sunbeams lay,
And bid them " *Take that gold and go away.*"

Anon a fevered change did come to me;
   And I went down beneath the surging waves;
Now riding on a dolphin, strange to see,
   And floating now along the mermaids' caves;
Straightway their coral grots would seem to be
   Changed in a moment to a world of graves,
And the loose sea-weed where I, tangling, fell,
To the long locks of gentle Isabel!

Anon a fevered change did come to me;
   And I went up upon the rushing wind;
Onward and onward soaring far and free
   Till one by one the stars were left behind;
Heaven burst upon my view, and I did see
   A *peri* fair in battle with a *fiend*
Who plunged her down. Oh, mercy! as she fell,
'T was that same shriek — " Edgar, *save Isabel!* "

Few scattered recollections yet remain
   Of forms that came and went I know not how,
And that my pillow gave my head less pain
   As if a mother smoothed it down but now;
Sometimes soft languor cooled my burning brain,

As if a sister's lips had kissed my brow,
But when my voice implored them not to fade
They all swept by, mocking my call for aid.

. . . .

Here let me pause — nor longer strive to sing
   The wayward wanderings of fantastic thought!
Vainly the minstrel wakes his trembling string
   To trace the vagaries of a mind o'erwrought.
Enough that sorrow lost at length its sting,
   And reason once again her empire sought,
As with a look of love and kiss of joy
His mother kneeled, and *knew* her "*dreaming boy.*"

THOU HAST WOOED ME WITH PLEDGES.

Thou hast wooed me with pledges
   A princess might wear;
Thou hast proffered rich jewels
   To wreathe mid my hair.
Ah! deck with thy treasures
   The halls of the sea;
Thy gold and thy purple —
   They are not for me.
But give me Love's myrtle
   And ribbon of blue;
And I'll go to the bridal
   At vespers with you.

Thou hast told of the glory
   Which waited thy bride;
Thy mansions of splendor,
   Thy lineage of pride.
Ah! show to the high-born
   Thy palace of glee;
Its courts and its titles —
   They are not for me.
But give me a cottage,
   A warm heart and true;
And I'll go to the bridal
   At vespers with you.

SHE WROTE.

She wrote upon the golden sand
    Where dashed the ocean's spray,
But fast as formed beneath her wand,
    The words were washed away.
And as she stood the shore beside,
    To watch the rising sea,
" 'T is ever thus," the maiden cried,
    " Oh, ever thus with me!
Upon this heart a picture bright
    Hope's pencil never drew,
But Sorrow came with waves of blight,
    And washed the lines from view."

She turned toward the setting sun
    To catch its vesper ray,
But while the light she gazed upon,
    It faded fast away.
And as the clouds with crimson dyed,
    She sadly stood to see,
" 'T is ever thus," the maiden cried,
    " Oh, ever thus with me!
A hand to mine I've never prest
    Whose clasp was not untrue,
And all that's bright, like yonder west,
    Hath proved as fleeting too."

STANZAS FOR MUSIC.

We have smiled and wept together,
    We have roamed by shore and sea,
We have stemmed misfortune's weather,
    Yet I part from thee.

Star of Love, how art thou clouding!
    Curtained shadows veil the sky,
In the storm my life-bark shrouding;
    Guide me with thine eye.

We have trod the mystic measure,
    We have sung the song of glee,
We have twined the wreath of pleasure,
    Yet I part from thee.

Sun of Hope, eclipsed in sorrow,
    Whither shall my footsteps stray?
Blind the night and bleak the morrow:
    Save me with thy ray.

THOU WERT NOT THERE.

Thou wert not there: from morn till night.
    All passion-tost. I chid the day:
For though the sun went down in light.
    The hours he marked still seemed to stay.
With lingering touch I swept the string.
    But vainly rang the whiling air;
Time hastened not his loaded wing. —
           Thou wert not there.

Thou wert not there this eye to see.
    To know the long. long watch it kept:
This eye whose light but shone for thee,
    Whose every tear for thee was wept.
It was not strange. for days and days
    Its glances roamed with vacant stare;
Thou wert not by to fix its gaze. —
           Thou wert not there.

Thou wert not there. though fever bound
    This throbbing brow with cords of flame.
And strangers heard. who lingered round,
    My wandering tongue pronounce thy name.
They watched my temple's deep'ning glow,
    They knew the grief I scarce could bear;
But *thou* who might'st have soothed that woe, —
           Thou wert not there.

MIDNIGHT.

WRITTEN AT WEST POINT.

It is the midnight hour. — the busy hum
   Of day is hushed, for man hath sunk to rest,
And the last echo of the evening drum
   Hath died long since far o'er the mountain crest:
No sound is heard, save when the deep winds come
   In fitful murmurs from the Hudson's breast,
Blending their whispers with the moaning breeze
   That wanders faintly through the forest trees.

The bird of eve is sitting on her bough
   Reciting to the stars her vesper hymn,
And the pale moon, as if to hear her vow,
   Floating from out the clouds, hath lit the limb
With heavenly lustre, and the earth, but now
   Shrouded with gloom as with a mantle dim,
Looks smiling forth through the effulgence bright,
   As if 't would say, How beautiful is night!

THE EYE OF CERULEAN BLUE.

The sun had just sunk in the west,
And the moon was just sinking there too,
And the clouds were the richest, the brightest, the best
By poet conceived or by painter expressed,
Yet I thought of no object, it must be confessed,
But her eye of cerulean blue.

I turned to the rose-colored sky,
As we spoke of its fast-fading hue,
But e'er we had gazed for a moment, a sigh
Came deep from my breast, and I dared not tell why —
How I dwelt, how I dreamed on the hue of her eye,
Her eye of cerulean blue.

We talked of the beauties of night,
Of a star just appearing in view.
And she thought that I spoke of *its* mild azure light,
When impassioned I swore 't was so lovely and bright;
But the star that *I* looked on, that dazzled my sight,
Was her eye of cerulean blue.

Her hand chanced to touch against mine;
('T was the softest that ever I knew,)
And she sighed like the breeze when 't is wooing
    the vine,
But the touch and the sigh were unanswered by
    mine,
For I felt and I saw but one object divine, —
Her eye of cerulean blue.

A wager I laid — should have won it —
On that eye of celestial hue,
But scarce had I written one stanza upon it,
When I saw it peep out 'neath its little brown
    bonnet,
And away went my heart, and away went my son-
    net:
Oh, that eye of cerulean blue!

LOVE AND REASON.

AN ALLEGORY.

One day when Love, oppressed with pain,
   Had laid aside his golden quiver,
And gone to cool his burning brain,
   To roam awhile by Reason's river;

Upon the bank of roses gay
   Which fringe the edge of Reason's water,
He saw a cherub girl at play,
   And knew the romp for Reason's daughter.

" Come hither, hither, blooming child!
   Long have I sought to have thee near me,
Let 's roam among these roses wild:
   I 've not my bow — you need not fear me."

As Love pronounced the maiden's name,
   From his bright wing he plucked a feather,
Pleased with the proffered toy she came,
   And hand in hand they roamed together.

At length there rose a tempest wild,
   Though Reason thought 't was not unpleasing,

But storms scarce felt by Reason's child,
 To gracile Love appear quite freezing.

"How shield me from this icy air!
 My wings are all too wet for flying —
Come, take me to that bosom fair,"
 Said Love to Reason, softly sighing;

And nestling up to Reason's form,
 Spread his chill wings on Reason's shoulder;
And this is why as *Love* grows *warm*,
 Reason, they say, grows *always colder*.

The Zephyr now rode down the air,
 To kiss the rain-drops from the cresses,
While Love unfolded Reason's hair,
 And dried his wings with Reason's tresses.

But Love grew faint and weary soon,
 As oft he grows by Reason's bowers,
So from the maid he asked the boon,
 To sleep that night among the flowers.

Reason replied with drooping head,
 And pausing 'neath a weeping willow,
She wove its branches for a bed,
 And plucked the rose-buds for a pillow.

But lest another storm might rise,
 Of which they 'd have too little warning,

One was to watch the changing skies,
   And one to sleep, by turns, till morning.

Thus each awhile in slumber lay,
   Each watched the other's couch of roses,
And this is why, they always say,
   When *Love awakes*, then *Reason dozes*.

I CANNOT LOVE HER.

I cannot love her; — every tress
　Which o'er her forehead strays,
Stamps on my soul, with deeper stress,
　The dream of other days.
Yet I have bowed beside her form
　In sorrow and in mirth,
With sigh and tear and pleading warm;
　Another gave them birth.

I cannot love her; — every glance
　Her eyes upon me cast
Serves but to strengthen and enhance
　The memories of the past.
Yet I have told her stars ne'er set
　In such deep lustrous blue,
And prayed her gaze one moment yet, —
　Ah! it was *Mary's* too.

I cannot love her; — cold and mute
　My heart to passion's spell,
Yet I have lingered o'er her lute,
　And praised its numbers well;
And whispered how an angel's tone
　Faltered its chords among,

And how her voice seemed passion's own, —
'T was thus that *Mary* sung.

Quench, quench this meteoric gleam,
  Mocking a planet's light!
Enough, — 't is past, — 't was but a dream, —
  Welcome, oblivion's night!
I *do not* love her; — 't were a spot
  Upon affection's sun:
I love but one — and she is not, —
  No! no! I love but *one*.

THE ISLE OF LOVE.

There 's a bright sunny spot where the cinnamon-
    trees
Shed their richest perfume to the soft wooing
    breeze ;
Where the rose is as sweet and as bright is the sky
As the balm of thy breath and the glance of thine
    eye ;
And clouds pass as soon o'er that beautiful isle,
As the tear on thy cheek disappears at thy smile.
Come, hasten, fair Emma, oh hasten with me
To that bright sunny spot in the far-distant sea.

Light breezes are swelling the gossamer sail
Of my love-freighted bark from the evergreen vale,
And loudly the night-bird is chanting her lay,
To shorten thy slumbers — away and away —
We will land mid the groves and each wild flower
    there
I will twine in a wreath for thy soft flaxen hair,
While we roam, like the antelope, reckless and free
O'er that bright sunny isle in the far-distant sea.

Soft music is there, for the mermaiden's shell
Is often heard winding through mountain and dell,

As the song of the sea-spirit steals to the shore
From the wave-girdled rock where the white billows
    roar ;
And the tones of *thy* voice, oh, how sweetly they'll
    blend
With the notes which the harps of the ocean nymphs
    send !
We will list to the strains as they float o'er the lea
Of that bright sunny spot in the far-distant sea.

Far, far, mid its bowers sequestered and lone
Young Love has erected a jessamine throne,
And sworn with an oath which no mortal may say
That none but the *fairest* its sceptre may sway.
Then hasten, fair Emma, oh hasten to-night,
While the stars are yet pale and the moon is yet
    bright ;
For, Love, he hath destined that sceptre for thee,
In that bright sunny isle in the far-distant sea.

BURNING LETTERS.

[CONCEIVE of a boarding-school miss, summoned by the paternal mandate, about to return to her friends. She has retired to her "boudoir" to reperuse her epistolary manuscripts and consign those to destruction which maidenly friendship would cherish, but which matronly prudence might condemn. Her eye lingers on them for the last time, as her fingers commit them one by one to the flames. We will follow her in song:] —

No! I'll not the thought recall!
Kindle, flame! consume them all, —
Every pledge of former years,
All my smiles and all my tears,
Letters traced by Friendship's fingers,
Lines o'er which my fancy lingers,
Every word and every name,
All must perish, — kindle, flame!
This! the first to meet thy rage —
How I've mused upon its page!
Ere the tender seal I tore,
Well I knew the stamp it bore;
Oh, the tales its face could tell!
Kindle, fire, and burn it well.
This! but yesterday it seems
Since it verified my dreams;
Days before my heart was sad,
Boding news of something bad;

When it came, alas how true!
Take it, fire! and burn it too.
Here is one oft read before:
Let me scan its lines once more.
Lovely writer, hath she deemed
I was happy as I seemed?
Had she only read my heart!
Bitter tears, why will ye start?
Ye have now no business here, —
Fire! 't is thine, burn high and clear!
Another and another yet;
This the tear hath often wet;
This came when my heart was gay,
Happy girl and happy day!
How my task I hurried o'er,
Once again to read it more!
This and this one night were brought,
When of home I fondly thought.
What my feeling who can say?
But the fire I cannot stay.
Last of all — here — take my last!
Burn it, flame, and burn it fast!
Melt the links of memory's chain,
Never to unite again;
Buried loves, and friendships true,
Fare ye well, — adieu! adieu!

STANZAS.

I saw thee when in humble sphere,
   Nor friends nor fortune round thee smiled,
And oft I shed the secret tear,
   That thou, alas, wert Sorrow's child.
'T was then thy youthful love I sought,
   But though my heart was knit to thine,
So wealth and pride o'er passion wrought,
   Never, I said, I'll call thee mine.

I saw thee when thy smile was bright,
   Leading the maze of Fashion's train;
I saw thee when thy step was light,
   Lending a charm to Music's strain.
But from the hour when *thou* wert blest,
   I marked *my* fortune's sad decline,
And though I loved thee, fondest, best,
   Then, then, oh ne'er I'd call thee mine.

Again our wayward stars have met,
   And now we *both* are sad and lone,
But dry the tear of past regret,
   The bridal voice shall claim its own.
Howe'er Misfortune's stormy blast
   May strive to make fond hearts repine,

The sundered chord unites at last:
　　Now, dearest love, I'll call thee mine.

Soft pillowed on that soothing breast,
　　This brow hath ached too long to know
There I may find that place of rest
　　The warring world would ne'er bestow.
And when our lives' declining star,
　　Obscured by death no more shall shine,
We'll wing our flight mid skies afar,
　　And still, dear love, I'll call thee mine.

VENUS OF CANOVA.

There is no cloud upon thy brow,
    Fair idol of a shrine above,
No gathering shadows round thee grow,
    Which veil the forms of earthly love.
O'er all that kneel in Beauty's bower
    Thou reignest still in queenly prime,
Thy life a never-ending hour,
    Unscathed by care, unmoved by time.

Yet none, whose lingering glances steal
    Along those lines of moulding rare,
But sigh to see and grieve to feel
    The loneliness of Beauty there.
Around thy lip's voluptuous swell
    Though all divine the smiles which play,
Yet where's the wildering breath to tell
    Its grief for pangs it could not stay?

Soft Pity looks with tearful eye,
    But pleads in vain to melt thine own;
The voice of Blood hath past thee by,
    What reck'st thou of its thunder tone?
Though withering Grief should league with Glee,
    Revenge forget his purpose bold,

And Hate turn back to gaze — *on thee*,
　　Thou 'dst heed it not — creation cold!

Why moulded thus serene and fair,
　　Pale image of a sculptor's dream?
Let *change* awhile be written there,
　　And lovelier far thy brow will seem.
Some line effaced by Sorrow's tear,
　　Some feature touched by dull Decay,
And thou shalt be an emblem dear
　　Of those we love that pass away.

TO IANTHE.

Since thou art gone, Ianthe,
Laughter hath lost its tone,
Smiles are like buds that wither,
    Since thou art gone.

Since thou art fled, Ianthe,
Music sits mute and lone,
For melody hath perished,
    Since thou art gone.

Since thou art gone, Ianthe,
Dimly the stars have shone,
Tears must have veiled their brightness,
    Since thou art gone.

Since thou art fled, Ianthe,
Love heeds not Beauty's throne,
For broken is her sceptre,
    Since thou art gone.

I LIVE FOR THEE.

I LIVE for thee — 't were little worth
   I know, such words the world to tell,
But yet the loveliest things of earth
   Repeat that phrase of pleasing spell.
The vesper bird, at close of day,
   Who greets his mate with songs of glee,
Does he not say, or seem to say,
             I live for thee?

I live for thee — the lute-string cries,
   Thou chosen of the minstrel band,
For one alone its music sighs,
   And answers not a stranger's hand.
The flower which marks the coursing sun,
   With constant gaze its god to see,
Oh! looks it not — thou glorious one —
             I live for thee?

I live for thee — bird, lute, and flower,
   Ah! weave again that soothing tone,
And waft it on to yon far bower,
   Where one ye know not sits alone.
And tell her how at even-tide,
   O'er tented plain or rolling sea,
Fond accents breathe — my gentle bride —
             I live for thee.

THE DYING BETROTHED.

MOTHER! raise my drooping head;
   Let the pure and placid sky,
Looking down upon my bed,
   Smile upon me e'er I die!
When the star of eve was bright,
   Gazing on its silver brow
I did love that vesper light:
   Let it shine upon me now.

Lift the curtain's jealous fold
   Where it intercepts the ray;
I have thought yon beams of gold
   Struggled on my couch to lay.
Ere they met my dying eyes
   Soft I dreamed some angel fair,
Watching o'er me from the skies,
   Sent them down to guide me there.

In the hour yon star grows pale,
   Then the pledge redeemed shall be;
Time nor distance may prevail, —
   'T was the sign *he* gave to me.
Look! it seemeth now to glide
   Sadly past yon sunset cloud;

Mother! like a soldier's bride,
    Dying in a crimson shroud.

Mother! hold in thine my hand,
    See how swiftly fades the day!
Let the breeze from battle land
    O'er my burning temples stray!
Music, like a cymbal's tone,
    Strangely rings upon my ear;
If it be his spirit-moan.
    Tell him that his bride is near.

Mother! but the tears which flow
    Down thy cheek. drop fast on mine;
Weep not, mother, that I go
    Where the stars forever shine!
Mid the sky that ne'er was dim,
    Far beyond the trumpet's swell,
Grieve not that I seek for *him!*
    Mother! mother! fare thee well!

IGNORANCE AND BEAUTY.

With cureless wound man's breast would smart,
  Pierced by that eye of blue,
Did not the tongue restore the heart,
  The eye might else undo.

FALSE GAYETY.

She hath decked her hair with a wreath of light;
  Those gems they are soft and clear,
For ere they slept mid her curls to-night,
  She washed them with a tear.

THE RESTLESS ONE.

SHE knew his brow was clouded,
   And she leaned it on her hand,
And gently wooed him to her side
   With breath like breezes bland.
But his eyes had caught a banner
   With its tassels flaunting wide,
And while he gazed upon its stars,
   They won him from his bride.

They lured him from the presence
   Of the cherished and the true,
No more to gaze upon her face,
   Her gentle smile to view;
And yet through life's long pathway,
   When the aisles of hope grew dim,
Bright as a deed of glory
   Was the smile she wore for him.

She knew they must be parted,
   Ere they had scarcely met,
And faster tear-drops dimmed her eyes
   That none but hers were wet.
And she wove a song of sorrow,
   Which she taught unto her lute, —

But the trumpet had a deeper charm,
   And the lover's lip was mute.

He left the song of Beauty,
   For the music of the plain,
The lowly breathing of the lyre,
   For pæans o'er the slain;
And yet that lyre, sweet-chorded,
   That voice like a mock-bird's tone, —
For him were garnered all its notes,
   For him it sang alone.

Time was Love's smile might conquer
   What the sword could ne'er alarm,
When strong was woman's lowly prayer
   As the might of the mailèd arm.
But the magic charm is over,
   And the siren voice is dumb,
While Love forsakes his gentle lute,
   For the roll of the daring drum.

THE CHILD'S REQUIEM.

Baby, sleep! serenely closing,
Droops thine eyelid's jetty fringe;
Death upon thy cheek reposing,
Slowly steals its vernal tinge.
   Though no father's voice may bless thee,
   Though no mother's arm caress thee,
   Never more shall grief distress thee,
             Baby, sleep.

Baby, sleep! in peace reclining,
Gently rests thy lowly head,
Angel faces brightly shining,
Smile above thy cradle-bed.
   Of the eye that weeps at waking,
   Of the heart that fills to breaking,
   Thou shalt never know the aching,
             Baby, sleep.

Baby, sleep! no morn of sorrow
Rises on thy night of pain;
Bright, though distant, is the morrow
When thy lip shall smile again.
   Till the hour — in clouds descending
   Comes the Judge, a world befriending,
   Mid hosannas never ending,
             Baby, sleep.

THE RETURN.

Joys that were tasted
   May sometimes return;
But the torch when once wasted,
   Ah! how may it burn!
Splendors now clouded,
   Ah! when will ye shine?
Broke is the goblet,
   And perished the wine.

Many the changes
   Since we last met,
Blushes have brightened,
   And eyes have been wet;
Friends have been scattered,
   Like roses in bloom;
Some at the bridal,
   And some at the tomb.

I stood in yon chamber,
   But *one* was not there;
Hushed was a lute-string,
   And vacant a chair.
Lips of love's melody,
   Where are ye borne?
Never to smile again,—
   Never to mourn.

IMPROMPTU

ON BEING ASKED TO WRITE SOMETHING DESCRIPTIVE OF THE EYES OF A CERTAIN COQUETTE, WHO WAS REPRESENTED TO BE A "VERY BEWITCHING CREATURE."

'T is well to discourse upon eyes of cerulean,
  Meek ones and mild ones, eyes lustrous and rich,
On the bright ones of Susan, the dark ones of Julianne,
  But what shall we say of the eyes that bewitch?

A difficult, dangerous subject to light upon,
  (However you view it, most surely it is,)
For those very same eyes which seem model'd to write upon,
  Are the last ones to languish and first ones to quiz.

THE LORE OF LOVE.

"Mother, what meant the sibil when
She bid me shun the gaze of men,
And said, while weeping 'neath the yew,
'Beware the hour of evening dew?'
The eye of youth is sweet to see,
It cannot lurk with harm for me;
And soft the eve with sunset red,—
The vesper hour I may not dread."

"Such warning dark, O daughter young,
Flows not alone from sibil tongue.
The strongest spell in Passion's bower
Is that which binds the twilight hour;
And eyes which seem of softest shade
Are those which look on love betrayed."

"And is it thus,—then, mother, why
Doth crimson crown the sunset sky,
And glances beam with azure light,
If full of danger, death, and blight?
Is maiden's heart a thing to grieve,
That Hope may mock, and Love deceive?"

"O daughter fair, go first explain,
Why floats the cloud and falls the rain,
With deep research next seek to know
Why green the leaf, and white the snow,
And, last of all, discover why
Both joy and grief should heave the sigh:
When these by Reason's rule ye prove,
Then may you learn the *lore of Love*."

THE LORE OF TEARS.

"Mother, why is it when I trace
The tear which falls on sister's face,
It seems to me so bright and fair
I almost wish 't was always there;
But when, sometimes, by soft surprise,
I 've caught the tear in father's eyes,
Those cherished orbs looked up so dim,
That, oh! I 've turned and wept with him?
Mother, I 'm but a maiden young, —
Inform my heart and teach my tongue."

"Come hither, child of tender years,
And learn of me the 'lore of tears.'
When sorrow pours, with drops that gleam,
On woman's cheek the crystal stream,
It is a sign by which to tell
The heart that aches will soon be well;
A measure kind which transient grief
Ordains to bring the heart relief;
A token that the mists of care
Will rise and leave the rainbow there.
But when the tears of woman weak
Are seen on manhood's hardy cheek,

They come, like heralds, to proclaim
The storm which shakes his thunder frame;
The struggle of the fires which burn
Within the bosom's heaving urn;
The effort of the tempest wave.
Heart-bound to burst its passion cave.
If e'er 't is thine, oh daughter fair,
To watch beside his brow of care,
By every tie which mercy forms,
Deal gently with that heart of storms."

THE OUTCAST.

They never more may breathe her name,
  That cherished name of gentle tone,
'T is blotted out in lines of shame
  On every page where once it shone.
Oh! may you never, never know
  The startling dream which haunts her rest,
Since that sad hour her conscious brow
  .Was lent to warm a faithless breast!

That brow, whose changing lines were such
  As charmed the wondering painter's view,
At which the master, gazing much,
  Forgot his easel as he drew;
The loftiest far among the proud,
  And loveliest still amid the fair,
No more shall tempt the glittering crowd
  To forge the chains they smiled to wear.

That voice, between whose words of guile
  Such witching tones of passion rung,
That Music's self would pause the while,
  Neglectful of the lute she strung,
No longer mid the tuneful choir
  Shall strive to wake the trembling lay,

Nor Love nor Friendship more aspire
  To sigh beneath its thrilling sway.

Yes! looks and words alike are vain;
  Though smiles may soothe and prayers may win.
They cannot break the galling chain
  Which binds the victim child of sin.
Like some frail bark upon the wave,
  Deserted by the idle air,
Not all the power which man may have
  Can burst the spell which keeps it there.

THE DISCARDED.

Is woman's love so lightly won,
    Obedient to call,
That like the lyre ye play upon,
    'T will change and sigh with all?
Go tell him from this hour we part,
    We own no mutual shrine, —
I will not brook another's heart
    Should share the joys of mine.

My step is light, my smile is gay,
    Nor yet my eye is dim, —
Go tell him how in halls I stray,
    And never think of him;
And how, at eve, when music's tone
    Comes gushing o'er the air,
I feel not in my bower alone,
    Nor miss his presence there.

I do not love, — I do not hate, —
    It were an idle thing!
In puling strain I will not prate,
    Nor yet the gauntlet fling;
But tell him, as some passing gleam
    That flits along the lea,

Or like a shadow on a stream,
  His memory is to me.

Perchance he thought, with simple guile,
  To prove me like a sword,
And hung with cunning craft the while
  Upon the stranger's word;
But tell him, when he left my side,
  I knew not that he went;
Nor shall I clothe my lip with pride,
  Nor sigh with discontent.

Ye voices soft, why o'er my heart
  Come with your promptings kind?
And has he tasted of the smart
  Which stings an anguished mind?
I care not for his troubled sleep, —
  Yet whisper in his ear,
My eye is not too proud to weep, —
  But *frozen* is the tear.

And tell him, though his every look
  Cold distance shuns to see,
Though like a falsely labelled book
  His name is now to me,
And though no more like music bland
  His voice may haunt my rest, —
I wear his jewel on my hand,
  His image on my breast.

LOVE'S PERFIDY.

"The waning moon with crescent pale
    Shines faintly o'er the lea,
My bark is near, and light the gale,
    Oh maiden, fly with me!
By all yon starry orbs I swear
    That thou my bride shall be!
Then trust my oath and hear my prayer,
    Oh maiden, fly with me."

"Though bright the evening sky awhile,
    Its hues will soon decay,
And oh! they say a lover's smile
    As soon will fade away.
The night is dark and lone the hour,
    And false the summer sea;
I cannot leave my greenwood bower,
    I cannot fly with thee."

"The summer rose may cease to blow
    Beside thy native rill;
That gentle stream may cease to flow
    Adown the distant hill;
Yon pine no more those walls may shade,
    And seared its leaves may be,

Yet still I'll love my mountain maid;
  Then maiden, fly with me."

Within the maiden's lonely bower
  Still blooms the summer rose;
Beside the castle's bannered tower
  That gentle stream still flows;
And o'er the turret's frowning height
  Yet rocks that forest tree, —
But ah! the maid hath wept the night
  She sought with Love to flee!

ROSALIE.

Alone, alone, my Rosalie !
She sleeps beneath the church-yard tree !
By yonder mound with daisies strewn ;
Her couch is there — alone — alone !
Lo ! yon dim star, whose lustre pale
Scarce struggles through its misty veil !
Each night, e'er yet its shining crest
Is cradled 'neath the burning west,
There comes a wild and lonely ray
To linger o'er her home of clay.
That star — that star — 't was in its gleam
We met, and mused by wood and stream ;
The witness lone of every sigh
We breathed beneath its presence high.
Oh ! then were hours of mystic sway
   Would suit the maze of numbers well,
Had minstrel words to weave the lay,
   Had minstrel strings the tones to tell.
Her heart was like the lava rock,
   Kindled at some Promethean ray,
Unmoved, save by Love's lightning shock,
   And yielding then — to melt away.
To love our souls gave equal birth,
   Each burned with simultaneous flame ;

One was the dross of sense and earth,
  And one was such as angels name.
I asked her not to be my bride,
  No prayers were breathed, no vows were sworn,
Yet were our souls so close allied
  I could not break the fetter strong.
Ah, Rosalie! my heart was true,
And yet my hand was not for you!
Thrice hapless hour I called thee mine,
  Of all thy after years the bane,
The dream of joy was deeply thine,
  And thine the anguish — thine the stain!
Too fragile dream — too hapless lot —
Yet would'st thou I had loved thee not?

As melts the cloud along the west,
  Her sunset smile went down on me,
As if her soul in joy caressed
  The parting pang which made it free.
While bending o'er that brow where oft
  My vigil heart had watched before,
When in the dream of rapture soft,
  Which it was doomed to know no more,
I saw a hand of hectic hue
Stamp on her cheek its signet true,
And by the flashing of her eye
I read the sign — my love must die!
I read! and dashed the tear aside
For her I ne'er had called my bride,

And wore a smile that none might know
My bosom's wilderness of woe.

But she, without a throb of pain,
    Smiled on and lingered still,
So calm and meek, that hope again
    Began my heart to fill;
As if the angel who was sent
    Her soul upon his wings to bear,
Paused o'er the spirit's monument,
    Enraptured with a mould so rare.

But when to kiss her dimpled mouth
The spring-breeze wandered from the south,
And when the buds, — be still my heart,
    Or break at once and drown my pain! —
The young buds swelled with quickening start,
    To dress for her their bloom again;
Just as appeared the first-blown flower,
As come to crown the bridal hour,
The shadowy cypress reared its head
Above her cold and dreary bed.
Alone, alone, my Rosalie!
She sleeps beneath the church-yard tree.

FRAGMENT.

Oft in the dream of night,
When sleep unfolds the curtained world to me,
Thine eye I meet, thy slender form I see,
Gliding by mossy rock and birchen tree,
    Through the dim vision light.

    Thy voice comes o'er my ear!
And its low music with a lute-like sound,
Prophetic hangs my boding heart around.
As erst 't was wont beside the far, far mound
    Where slept the forest deer.

THE DYING PENITENT.

The winds that in the morn had slept,
   Now gently stole adown the lea,
To murmur where Eliza wept,
   Beside the lonely trysting tree.
But though serene the sigh which swayed
   Those bosoms of the viewless air,
Each breath but caused a deeper shade
   To veil the brow which languished there.

Then, soft, like ocean's tenderest moan,
   Which grief through tears would smile to hear,
There came a wave of gurgling tone,
   With strains to glad Eliza's ear;
But vainly bears that gentle wave,
   Rich melodies from ocean's grot, —
Not all the tones the sirens have,
   May soothe the pang which sleepeth not.

Just then, from out the dying day
   Fast sinking down the west, a streak
Of golden sunset chanced to stray,
   And trembled on Eliza's cheek.
"Oh! pledge of Hope, too brightly given,
   I weep no more," the frail one cried,
And gazing on that type of Heaven,
   The lone Eliza smiled — and died.

THE FOREVER LOST.

Along thy features, wan with care,
  My earnest glances turn to dwell,
Although I read depictured there
  What once my lips had clung to tell.
The clouded type of one I trace
  Who sought the rose, but plucked the rue;
Whose constant tear may ne'er efface
  The burning deed she sighed to do;

Of one who toyed with Passion's spell,
  Till lost beneath the wildering wave;
Of one pale Virtue weeps to tell,
  The victim child she could not save.
As gleams at morn the dew-bright gem,
  So once thy bud of fortune shone,
But shaken from the parent stem,
  Now scorned and crushed it droops alone.

And yet not all unblest to thee
  The boon thy heart quailed not to give;
That waning cheek a sign shall be,
  Toward which frail youth may look and live.
To treacherous seas, when storms are past,
  Soft winds may woo with temptings fair,

But he who sees the shattered mast
　　Not soon forgets the danger there.

Oh ! shadowy dream of transient bliss !
　　Why come ye thus in semblance mild,
With Faith's low phrase and Love's soft kiss,
　　To lure from heaven its thoughtless child ?
Where'er, henceforth, your altars glow,
　　Far let their warning beacons shine,
That all the perjured spot may know,
　　Where Falsehood rears her faithless shrine.

MATILDA.

And thou art faded like a ray
   Which melts upon the sight!
I thought to gaze upon the day,
   But look upon the night.
The hope that rose, a falcon fair,
   Floats by on idle wing;
The dove that smote the morning air
   Hath proved a vanished thing.

Where art thou, sister of my heart,
   Where art thou in thy mirth?
Come, and fulfil thy wonted part
   Beside our father's hearth.
I stand within thy chamber where
   Last thrilled thy laughing tone;
I cannot brook that vacant chair,
   Sister, where art thou gone?

I thought to hear thy song elate
   Resounding from my home,
To meet thee bounding to the gate,
   As thou wert wont to come.
I find the lute within thy bower,
   But not the hand to play,

How dreary seems the sunset hour!
    Why art thou thus away?

The cloth is laid, the board is spread,
    Come to thy brother's call!
Yon echo, answering to my tread,
    Sounds lonely through the hall.
Come, with thy prattling voice of love,
    And with thy smile of cheer;
The house seems chill and sad the grove,
    Sister, thou art not here.

Yes, thou art faded, like a ray
    Which melts upon the sight;
I thought to gaze upon the day,
    But look upon the night.
Thy spirit form hath stretched its wing,
    And left my hearth alone;
Thy spirit voice, where angels sing,
    Awakes its angel tone.

Above thy bower the tresseled vine
    Once more the dew may wet,
The sun within thy chamber shine
    As though he ne'er had set;
The bird return unto the tree,
    The fold unto the plain,
All be revived in turn — but thee:
    Thou shalt not come again.

THE DESERTED BRIDE.

'T is past the hour of evening prayer,
   What lonely watch is mine!
I hear thy step upon the stair,—
   No, no, it is not thine.
'T was but a sound the tempest made
Along the moaning balustrade.

What circean spells, what siren charms,
   What words of secret art,
Thus keep thee from my longing arms,
   Oh partner of my heart!
And am I not thy chosen bride,
The flower that blooms but at thy side?

Soft words may fall from lips refined,
   From eyes soft glances shine,
But mid the crowd thou may'st not find
   A heart which loves like mine.
The very tear thy coldness brings
Seems welcome, since for *thee* it springs.

Have I not smiled when thou wert gay,
   Wept did thy look reprove,

Loved thee as *woman* sometimes may,
   As *man* can never love?
All this — yea more, 't was mine to give,
And unrequited — lo! I live.

Yet thou did'st once with accents bland
   Beside me bend the knee,
And swear in truth this little hand
   Was more than worlds to thee.
This jeweled hand — what is it now?
The *token of a broken vow.*

Oh, love! how oft the bridal ring
   Binds fast its golden tie,
To make the heart a slighted thing
   Ye pass unheeded by!
The charm is broke — the spell is gone —
And conscious woman weeps alone.

THE DEAD MOTHER.

" She sleeps — how long she sleeps — the sun hath sunk beneath the west,
And risen twice, yet still she keeps that deep and quiet rest.
Why did they stand beside her couch and weep with such ado?
Come hither, brother; thou and I will gaze upon her too.
Yet stay, we will not go there yet — but let us wait until
The sinking sun again hath set — and all around is still,
Except the spirit-winds which rise like wailings on the air,
Then will we step in silence forth and gaze together there.

" Sister, tread softly ! "
      " Hark, that sound ! "
          " 'T is but the midnight hour
Slow tolling deep and heavily, from yonder distant tower !
Come hither, sweet, nor stay thy step howe'er thine eye may swim,

'T is but the dull sepulchral lamp which makes its
    vision dim.
Nay, sister, tremble not, — 't is true the time *is*
    lone and drear,
And fitfully the taper flares that lights us to the
    bier;
But thou did'st breathe in earnest tones the mourn-
    ful wish but now,
To come at midnight hour and gaze upon thy
    mother's brow.
This is the hour — and we have passed along the
    silent hall,
And here, as by the dead we stand, I lift aside
    the pall,
And here the coffin's lid I move — while thus I
    raise the veil,
Turn, gentle sister, turn and look upon her features
    pale!
Stoop down and kiss the pallid cheek, though cold
    and damp it be,
Which in the hour of song and mirth so oft was
    pressed by thee,
And clasp in thine the lifeless hand stiff folded on
    the breast,
Whose pulses warm were wont to lull thy infant
    brow to rest!"

"I hear thy words, my brother dear; I 'm leaning
    o'er the spot;
And do I see a parent's face? alas! I know it not.

What! *this* my mother? No, oh no, not this on
    which I gaze;
Her eyes were bright, like angel's eyes, but these are
    dim with glaze;
Her lips were smiling, like the sky which never
    knew a cloud,
But these are silent, cold and pale, — pale as the
    winding shroud.
They told me that she only slept, and that she still
    was fair
As when her hand of snow-drop lay against her
    raven hair.
But as I gaze upon this cheek, there lies a shadow
    deep,
And on the brow a fixedness they never wore in
    sleep;
While for the purple vein, I trace a line of dark decay, —
No! this is not the form I loved, this ghastly thing
    of clay!"

THE LUTE AND SHELL.

Sing mournfully, sing mournfully,
   The lute hath lost a string;
I heard the snapping of the chord
   Which never more will ring.
All trembling 'neath some careless hand,
   Deep thrilled, and died the strain;
Sing mournfully, sing mournfully, —
   'T will never wake again!

Strike, strike the lyre with gladder sound!
   A shell of brilliance rare
Is brought from Ocean's farthest bound
   To blaze in Beauty's hair.
But ah! some chisel's heedless touch
   Hath dimmed its changing hue:
Sing mournfully, sing mournfully, —
   That shell is broken too.

Oh! ye who toy with gentle Love,
   Treat, treat him kind and well;
One careless look and he may prove
   Like shattered lute and shell.
One heedless word may quench the light
   Of smiles which *so* did shine;
Then mournfully, sing mournfully, —
   A broken *heart is* thine.

I COME TO THY PRESENCE.

I come to thy presence
  To worship and woo,
With none to befriend me,
  Undaunted I sue ;
I care not, thou fair one,
  So thee I may win,
For suitors without,
  Or for guardians within.

The long-buried secret,
  Now, now I impart,
The chain of thy beauty
  Hath worn to my heart.
The tones to make happy
  Thy lips ever bear
Have haunted my bosom
  Like shadow and care.

Oh! bright but untried one,
  Hear not with disdain ;
Thy smile is my pleasure,
  Thy frown is my pain.
But speak, and I care not,
  So thee I may win,
For suitors without,
  Or for guardians within.

MY BOSOM IS A SEPULCHRE.

My bosom is a sepulchre
    Where Sorrow loves to stay;
A shadow lies upon my heart,
    And will not flit away.
In vain the proffered word of cheer,
    Or tone of music deep;
My bosom is a sepulchre,
    Where Sorrow loves to weep.

Life's natal star shone joyously,
    'T was like a sun to me;
But e'er the twilight left the sky,
    It set beneath the sea.
No suppliant look may call it back,
    Nor word of pleading prayer, —
My bosom is a sepulchre,
    And Hope is buried there.

Speak not of forms affectionate,
    Of flowers whose hues are fled,
For Hope to me is like the rose
    Which bloometh with the dead.
Oh! what unto that icy brow
    The perfume of the leaf?
My bosom is a sepulchre
    For buried Hope and Grief.

THE RED ROSE; OR, PRIDE REPROVED.

A RED rose hung upon a tree,
A rose 't was passing fair to see,
Half shrinking from the morning ray,
With blushes soft as dying day.
A maid who trod the early dew
Espied that rose of sunset hue,
And 'raptured with its beauty rare,
Purloined it for her shining hair.
"Sweet flower," exclaimed the girl, "to-night
I 'll twine thee mid my ringlets bright,
And not a brow, whose cinctures shine
With gems of cost, shall vie with mine."

But when at length pale evening came,
To veil with shadows sunset's flame,
When the last beams of light withdrew,
The rose with day had faded too.
Too late the maid bewailed the hour
For sake of self she plucked the flower.
While to the spot her fancy clung,
Where breathing sweet at morn it hung,
With altered look and tone of grief,
She murmured o'er the drooping leaf:

"I thought with thee, oh rose of day,
To rule the night with haughty sway,
Where, mistress of the crowded room,
'T was mine to smile, and thine to bloom.
But ah! a lesson meet for pride,
I have but wept — and thou hast died."

STANZAS FOR MUSIC.

I met thee in the dance, love,
   I saw thine eye of light,
And oh! its every glance, love,
   Will haunt my couch to-night.
Thou mournest for the weed, love,
   Which withers mid thy hair,
But little wilt thou heed, love,
   The tale my lips declare.

Thy gentle voice I heard, love,
   I hung upon its tone,
And oh! thy every word, love,
   Was soft as music's own.
The swan is on the stream, love,
   The linnet on the spray;
Come, where the billows gleam, love,
   And listen to my lay.

I weave a mystic wreath, love,
   Thou know'st, and only thou;
'T is fragrant as thy breath, love,
   'T is stainless as thy brow.
I cast it where thy feet, love,
   Will roam beside the sea,
To breathe in language sweet, love,
   Of him who lives for thee.

NEW ORLEANS, *May*, 1838.

THE EAGLE AND DOVE.

'T is the bird of Jove's thunder!
  'T is the wing of Love's joy!
Why roam ye together,
  Thou fierce one and coy?

In the path of the lightning
  Ye traverse the sky,
What hold ye in union
  Oh low one and high?

Through clouds ye float proudly,
  But, weak one, beware!
Thy pinions once weary,
  Thy home is not there.

'T is the sky for the mighty!
  'T is the spray for the small!
Low bird with the lofty,
  Come back ere ye fall.

Oh, look at Love's picture,
  I draw at your side!
Ill-matched from the altar
  Goes bridegroom and bride.

One proud and high-titled,
  And stern to reprove;
One meek, but undowered,
  And born but for love.

Together — together
  They speed on their flight, —
They float through life's ether,
  That dark one and bright, —

Till chilled and benighted,
  Unskilled thus to fly,
The wing of that gentle one
  Fails in the sky.

SUWANEE SPRINGS, *Florida.*

THE BRIDE'S PRAYER.

Father! I come to Thee, a handmaid weak,
    Whose lips have scarcely breathed their bridal vow.
But, bathed in tears, Thy holy shrine I seek,
    For shadowy care sits heavy on my brow.

In gifts of love though manifold Thou art,
    One prayer I word, one only boon I crave, —
He leaves me, Father, tears me from his heart;
    Watch, bless, and guide him o'er the pathless wave.

I suffer for his sake; — these vigil eyes
    Grow heavy with a sense of outward weight;
Too deeply have I gazed upon the skies,
    Scanning the burning star which rules his fate.

I tempt Thee with an offering; — Father, look
    With kindness on me, — listen to my prayer!
My heart such anxious throbbing may not brook,
    Sinking it is with doubt and dark despair.

This, the sole offspring of our mutual love,
    O'er whose soft smile these watching eyes grow dim,
Father, if *Thee* love's sacrifice can move,
    My arms present, oh, wild exchange! for him.

Shield, shield him from the tempest when its wing
  With restless wandering sweeps his ocean bed,
When round his couch mad waves hope's death-
    knell ring,
  And heaving billows lift his tossing head.

Have mercy on him, Father, — if I weep
  It is but woman's tear, — I trust in Thee;
Let from the cloud which thunders o'er the deep
  Thy rainbow smile beam down and calm the sea.

Whate'er his sins, blot out or call *them mine*,
  So thou uphold'st him on the crested wave:
The prayer of love, of faith, ascends thy shrine, —
  I kneel, I plead, I wrestle, — Father, save!

DREAM OF THE BETROTHED.

Wipe off the anguish from my brow,
  Damp with the dews of pain,
Father, I had a dream but now
  Which must not come again.
Mid crowded aisles I seemed to stand,
  Decked as they deck a bride,
They placed a ring upon my hand
  And took me from thy side.

I breathed the censor's fragrance where
  The clouded incense fell,
I heard amid the chanted prayer
  The organ's lordly swell;
And oh! my bosom heaved the sigh
  Which rapture loves to wake —
But when I caught my father's eye,
  Methought my heart would break.

With wreaths of love from myrtles wrought,
  To bind my hair they came,
And many a gentle lip was fraught
  With phrases sweet to name;
But when thy brow, eclipsed in woe,
  Like twilight o'er me shone,

I thought it was unkind to go,
    And turned — and wept alone.

Yet to these eyes in tears upraised
    They gave but little heed,
They beckoned where the torchlight blazed,
    And bade the bridegroom speed.
I saw him kneeling at my feet,
    His words were low the while,
But though his smile was passing sweet,
    'T was not *my father's* smile.

He told of joys which rapture wove
    Beneath the bridal vine,
And bowers which breathed with sighs of love —
    Oh, sweeter far than thine.
But, father, press me to thy heart,
    So throbs my brow with pain, —
That dream — ah! would it bid us part? —
    It must not come again.

TO ADA.

O THOU, whose eyes of pensive light
    Like sunset skies were born to shine!
Thou art not by to gild the night
    Of one whose spirit clings to thine.
Adown thy cheek the tear may stray,
    He cannot kiss the crystal dim;
Thy tiny lip may learn to pray,
    He cannot hear the prayer for him.

To glad my brow, they tell me oft
    That thou art happy far from me,
But in the hour of slumber soft
    I only dream I live for thee.
By morn and eve, thou hallowed part
    Of one affection holds most dear,
I only feel where'er thou art,
    Thou art not here — thou art not here.

Think not thy name abroad I fling
    To court remark from idle tongue,
I did but breathe it o'er the string
    When soft and fast the numbers rung.
The hour will come when thou may'st learn —
    Perchance and love — thy father's strain;

And wilt thou chide he so did yearn
   To clasp his cherished child again?

Once o'er my hopes a vision wrought:
   To watch thy growth I seemed to stand,
While, through the glass which Fancy brought,
   I saw thee bloom beneath my hand.
And it was sweet to feel the while,
   Indulging in that mood of air,
How oft thy lip with tender smile
   More than repaid a father's care.

Alas! that dream of heavenly ray
   No longer now its radiance sheds,
Where bright its path of glory lay,
   The phantom Future darkly treads.
And ah! that glass which showed mine eye
   An image like the rainbow fair —
The wing of Change hath swept it by,
   And left the storm-cloud sleeping there.

But yet the power which gave me birth
   In grace perhaps this meed hath given;
Too long I might have clung to earth,
   Perchance have thought too late of heaven;
And by the angel earthward sent,
   To bid me hence, it might be told
He found my spirit well content,
   Twining a daughter's locks of gold.

HUMMOCK, *Okee-fee-nokee Swamp,*
   Jan. 29th, 1839.

THE CONSTANT ONE.

It was the soft and dreamy hour
   When hearts replete with love's excess
Too deeply feel its dangerous power,
   Nor yet, spell-bound, would wish it less.
A voice, with tones to music dear,
   Sang softly mid the twilight dim,
While one stood by, the words to hear,
   Which tell-tale Echo stole for him.

"Oh, bear from hence my shattered lyre,
   I cannot wake its passion-tongue,
The hand may mend a broken wire,
   But who shall tune a heart unstrung?
The lay my voice was tuned to sing
   One heart alone can draw from me;
I wind a wreath, I wear a ring, —
   But not for thee, no, not for thee.

"My lips were taught in days of yore
   A simple strain they thrilled to tell,
Those witching words they breathe no more,
   But who shall break that silent spell?
Love launched a bark of fairy form
   Upon my bosom's restless sea,

It liveth yet amid the storm, —
   But not for thee, no, not for thee.

"I know that eye which on me turns
   Is fixed beneath a wild'ring spell,
I know that tongue impassioned burns
   To word a thought 't is vain to tell ;
I know what shadow dims thy brow,
   And yet, and yet unkind in me,
I breathe a prayer, I lisp a vow, —
   Still not for thee, no, not for thee."

Died down the sky the blush of day,
   As soft the mournful music rang,
While Echo still was heard to say
   The sad'ning words the siren sang ;
And ever thus the sounding string
   Was answered by the tell-tale lea,
"I wind a wreath, I wear a ring, —
   But not for thee, no, not for thee."

THE LAST LOOK.

She wept beside the couch of him
   Who won her bridal vow,
While Death, like ray of starlight dim,
   Slept palely on his brow.
Unto thy side once more I come
   Bird-like to find my nest;
The weary turtle seeks the home
   She built upon thy breast.

I cannot bear to live away
   From that dear smile of light,
Too sadly drags the long, long day,
   Too lonesome wears the night.
How shall I bide the world's bleak storm,
   When its tempest shakes my heart?
Ah me, give back these kisses warm;
   We may not — *cannot* part!

But hist! what freezing thoughts restrain
   The words I fain would speak?
I dare not touch thy hand again,
   I dare not press thy cheek.
Cold, cold! — sweet love, is this the spot
   Thou gav'st me at thy side?

Ah no, this pulseless breast is not
  The pillow of thy bride.

And yet the lip of softened mould
  Seems such as once was thine;
Nay, nay, I dream, 't is clammy cold,
  And answers not to mine.
It breathes no word of soothing tone,
  It wears no smile for me, —
And as I gaze, I feel alone,
  I feel alone with thee.

The spirit light, whose flame divine
  Burns not by human will,
Hath vanished from its earthly shrine,
  And left the temple chill.
While shadowy phantoms from above
  Sigh on the darkened air,
"Ye look not on the form ye love, —
  'T is Death who sleepeth there."

THE MAIDEN'S HEART.

If you should twine a garland green,
   A wanton hand the wreath might spoil;
If you should paint a rosy screen,
   A careless touch the leaf might soil;
From the rare chain which Memory keeps
   Some cherished link may still be lost;
And yet the tear which Sorrow weeps
   Be bright, with grief of little cost.

If you should roam along the sand,
   Your foot may break a crystal rare;
If you should delve in treasure land,
   Your axe may crush a brilliant fair;
If you should fill a goblet bright,
   Some slip may make the draught in vain;
And yet — still yet — 't were matter light,
   But little loss or little gain.

But as you pass life's varied streams,
   Should you observe, with eyes that rove,
A pearl of price which softly gleams,
   Deep fixed in woman's breast of love,
Oh, by the words of mystic art
   Which o'er the lyre imploring ring,
Guard well that gem — 't is maiden's heart —
   Nor deem the toy an idle thing.

THE SCARCE FORGOTTEN.

They met while through the chamber
    Soft floated music rare,
The self-same charm was on her cheek
    As oft had lingered there;
Gladness was in her glances,
    Softness was in her tone,
And yet her image from his breast
    With all its joy had gone.

Her burning glance was on him,
    Yet past he idly by,
The rose-hue changed not on his cheek
    Beneath that conscious eye;
Still an early dream came o'er him,
    Of mingled love and pride:
He saw the idol of his youth,
    And he saw another's bride.

The whirling dance wove mazes
    Wherein her feet kept time,
Her sailing step went down the hall,
    To the sound of the measured chime;
But he heeded not her motion,
    And he never praised nor blamed;—

Pray what had *his* weak words to do
    With what *another* claimed?

They met as meets the stranger
    Without a smile or frown;
Yet dimly shining through the past
    Did Memory's star look down;
While softly siren fingers
    Touched a forgotten string,
As striving with a spectre strain
    To raise a vanished thing.

Love's cloud which so did lower
    When its lightnings pierced his breast,
Like wanton waves when winds go down,
    Hath gone long since to rest;
And the mystic thought, which bound him
    Strong as a mortal tie,
Slow fading through the mist of years,
    At length hath floated by.

STANZAS.

I see thee not, I hear thee not,
  I stand not at thy side,
I miss thy presence in the morn
  And at the eventide.
Ill boding to the fortune dark
  Which prompts me still to rove;
I see thee not, I hear thee not,—
  Where art thou, O my love?

The word to me seemed very dear
  Which bound thee to my heart,
But ah! it proved a mocking sound,—
  We only met to part.
Some lip it was of evil charm
  Which blessed and called us one;
I see thee not, I hear thee not,—
  Sweet love, where art thou gone?

Though pleasant, in the sunset glow,
  To sit mid rustling limes,
I languish for the sky of snow,
  And star of other climes;
Through orange groves the wind is sweet,
  And soft the southern air,

But when the northern storm-clouds meet,
  My wandering thoughts are there.

It often seemeth to mine eye
  My lot is rudely cast,
Too few my glimpses of the sky,
  Too many of the blast;
It may not be, — I only know,
  However vain to tell,
I see thee not, I hear thee not, —
  Loved one and lost, farewell!

FLORIDA, 1837.

THE LONELY GRAVE.

She resteth where the flashing stream
    Flits fast along the shore,
But in that sleep without a dream
    She heareth not its roar;
Above her grave wild roses bloom,
    In summer's gentle hours,
But not a hand is near that tomb,
    To train its drooping flowers.

Lone, watching by her silent bed,
    The squirrel oft is seen;
Wild ivy, too, grows o'er her head,
    And moss and myrtles green;
And in the night the wind's deep sigh
    Is heard along the air,
As if in faint inquiry why
    So still she slumbereth there.

With threads of lint a plaintive bird
    Hath braided there its nest,
While all day long its voice is heard
    Above her pulseless breast,
Until pale eve, at close of day,
    In sadness and alone,

Draws near to gild with pensive ray
  That grave without a stone.

It was a gentle girl, they said,
  Whose lover broke her heart,
And at her own request was laid
  Far from her friends apart.
She gave him all her maiden store,
  To light his bosom dim,
And when, alas! she had no more,
  She could but die for him.

FOREVER THINE.

Forever thine! though land and sea divide us,
      Forever thine;
Though burning wastes and winds — whate'er betide us,
      Forever thine;
Mid dazzling tapers in the marble alley,
      Forever thine;
Beneath the evening moon in pastoral valley,
      Forever thine;
And when the feeble lamp of life, expiring,
      Ceases to shine,
My soul will echo — echo, still retiring,
      Forever thine!

SHE LOVES ANOTHER.

She loves another! — I have learned
    The lore of womankind;
The hope which in my bosom burned
    Was idle as the wind;
I would not see her Parian brow,
    Her name I would not hear,
The lips which breathed a hollow vow —
    How can I hold them dear?

She loves another! — had I deemed
    Aught could ensue like this,
When first with trusting faith I dreamed
    How she was framed for bliss,
I might have quenched the inward glow
    Which thrills my bosom yet,
Nor rashly taught this heart to know
    What it would fain forget.

She loves another! — he is dear
    Whose name she shunned to speak;
His faltering tones are in her ear,
    His kiss is on her cheek.
'T is well, 't is right, — serene and bright
    Their future hours may be,
But joy, methinks, should first unite
    Faith and Inconstancy.

    Fort Mellon, *Florida.*

STANZAS.

It is the hour of mirth and wine,
   Deep sleeps the field, the watch is set;
Since thou hast taught me to repine,
   Oh Fortune, teach me to forget!
What boots it for this wandering eye
   To roam where recollection lives?
Oh, drain the stream of Lethe dry,
   Or cure the wound which Memory gives!

I had a hope which came and past;
   I had a dream, — that, too, is o'er;
The bark in which I braved the blast
   Struck rudely on a surf-beat shore;
Forgetful of the tempest's shock,
   It sought the sea on breezes fair;
I stand alone upon the rock,
   Gazing upon the shipwreck there.

In slumber's hour — while yet a boy —
   Oft to my couch a Spirit came,
And there it sang with notes of joy,
   Like Rapture o'er a wind-harp's frame;
And it was then my heart's belief
   Some siren sweet from heaven was there,

But now I think 't was shadowy Grief,
  Who wore the garb which Joy should wear.

And once a star — a single star,
  One of a group and one of three —
Seemed, as I watched its light afar,
  To live for me, and only me;
I do not know the mystic power
  Which bade me think it so should shine;
But hours like this — the midnight hour —
  Its eye seemed ever turned to mine.

And oft I thought, in Fancy's dream,
  It looked so pure, it shone so fair
While gazing on its liquid gleam,
  An angel's face was buried there;
Since years are mine and wisdom's lot,
  I know how wild such fancies were,
Yet little boast to know I 'm not
  The object of an angel's care.

STANZAS TO MARY.*

I know a change is on thy cheek,
  Although I see it not,
And that the home thy longings seek
  Is now a distant spot;
I know my lyre of murmurs deep
  For thee hath shadows dim,
And thou wilt turn aside to weep,
  To weep, alas! for *him*.

But thou art learned in music's art
  And measured numbers well,
And know'st the voice which pains the heart
  Still soothes it with its spell;
So sad and soft with chosen word
  I wake my dreary strain,
And gently touch the mournful chord,
  To chant thy lover slain.

No muffled drum with note of woe
  Proclaimed when he was dead,
No funeral flag with solemn show,
  Half-mast, the tidings sped,

---

* Written for Mrs. Col. Thompson, whose husband was killed at the battle of the Okeechubbe, Fla., December 25, 1837.

But fierce and far, from bank to bank,
  Broke forth a savage yell,
And the soldier in the rearmost rank
  Knew that a warrior fell.

Oh, 't is a mournful thing to be
  Amid the battle blast,
And o'er a brow we love, to see
  The death-tint stealing fast!
To view the all-unconscious glance
  Fixed in a vacant stare,
And yet the banner on the lance,
  And the trumpet on the air!

Thou wert not there to see him die
  Upon the warring heath;
Thou wert not there to close his eye
  And watch his parting breath, —
To feel his fingers' quivering touch,
  His last, last look to see;
And he whom thou did'st love so much
  Was buried far from thee.

In vain his lip of anxious care
  Soft murmured "Mary, come;"
Thou did'st not hear that lowly prayer
  The exile breathed for home;
And when upon the crimson sand,
  Mid shout and thunder peal,
He stretched for thee his dying hand,
  It grasped a thing of steel.

Oh, in the hour Death's angel came
   Life's loosened chord to break,
Upon thy bosom's conscious frame
   Did not a heart-string shake?
How could *his* spirit leave its goal
   Upon that fearful day,
And *thine* not feel the pang which stole
   Thy more than life away?

Thy heart is now a desert spot,
   Where joy hath ceased to bloom,
Yet thine the hope which sleepeth not,
   But shines beyond the tomb;
Though burst the coil of mortal birth,
   'T is not forever riven,
The spirit which so loved on earth
   Yet lives and loves in heaven.

DEATH OF THE IMPROVISATRICE.

TRIBUTE TO " L. E. L."

" She died
Like a pale flower nipt in its sweet spring-tide,
Ere it had bloomed."
ELLEN ARTORE'S EPITAPH, *written by herself.*

I.

Sing, minstrel, sing the bier
Where rayless she doth lie,
Like morn's bright dewy tear,
Crushed by rude footsteps ere
    The sun is high.

II.

Lift up the jealous veil
Which so doth interpose
To hide the finger pale
That smote (oh, sound of wail!)
    Love's bosom rose.

III.

Let music's deepest swell
Echo the chord along,
While sad its murmurs tell,
How faded and how fell
    That flower of song.

IV.

Sing, minstrel, pour thy lay!
The lyre's best string is mute;
Chant the young Queen of May,
Whose hand forgets to stray
      Along the lute.

V.

Sing to the breezes how,
Caressing and caressed,
Like stream from mountain brow
To placid lake below,
      She sank to rest.

. . . . .

VI.

And the deep-voiced minstrel spoke!
She has left her spirit height,
Like tree 'neath woodman's stroke,
Like bird with pinion broke,
      In midway flight.

VII.

She hath faded down the sky,
Singing such melting tone,
That the wild lark hovering high,
To catch that melody,
      Forebore its own.

VIII.

Too cold the world's bleak shower
Upon her cheek of pearl,

And like the passion-flower,
Chilled in ungenial bower,
        So drooped the girl.

IX.

Death saw, and loved the maid —
Oh, gem for dark decay! —
And with a kiss of shade,
All Judas-like, betrayed
        The prize away.

X.

Along the silent stair,
So stealthy was his tread,
That the watchers, worn with care,
Dreamed not of robber there,
        Till he had fled.

XI.

And the watch-lamp, flick'ring dim,
Cast o'er the mould he left
Shadows with mantles grim —
Phantoms in league with him —
        To hide the theft.

XII.

But when the garish day
Shone out from orb divine,
They read, by the tell-tale ray
Which bathed that cheek of clay,
        The Spoiler's sign.

XIII.

They knew that she had died,
That the archer's claim was paid,
Yet one who stood beside
That remnant of a bride,
        Almost had said,

XIV.

" How beautifully deep
In love's fond trance she lies!
It is a sin to weep,
So gently closes sleep
        Her soft-sealed eyes!"

THE CLOUD AND STREAM.

There was a cloud at even
  So spiritually fair,
Methought some creatures of the sky
  Had raised their mansion there;
And when its fleecy bosom
  Gleamed in the hallowed light,
They said it was an angel's wing
  That made its hues so bright.

There flowed a stream of summer
  So lovely from its spring,
The merest waif upon its breast
  Became an envied thing;
And in the starry midnight
  So gleamed its mirror tide,
The very sea-nymphs left their caves
  To revel at its side.

But ah, soon failed the sunlight,
  Failed too the fountain's head;
That cloud became an Ethiop spot,
  A waste that river-bed.
Hope of the youthful bosom,
  Boyhood's aspiring dream,
How like are ye, in Reason's eye,
  Unto that cloud and stream!

Fort Gilmer, *Florida.*

COME WHERE THE BILLOW HEAVES.

Come where the billow heaves, love,
    Along the silver grain!
Moonlight is on the leaves, love,
    And the zephyr fans the plain;
Morn with its garish light, love,
    May shine for colder bowers,
But the soft and gentle night, love,
    Was made for climes like ours.

Come where the clasping vine, love,
    Was trained to shade thy brow,
That not a lip save mine, love,
    Should marvel at its snow;
An evergreen its name, love,
    To typify thy youth;
'T is fragile like thy frame, love,
    But constant like thy truth.

In days of old, verse tells, love,
    With charms how music wrought;
But woman knows of spells, love,
    Which music never taught.
Come to the moonlight plain, love,
    Out in the perfumed air,
Hearts have a mystic chain, love,
    Which bind them closer there.

NEW ORLEANS, *May* 20, 1840.

SONG.

To wake her lute, which long had slept,
   She held it in the breath of Spring,
But when the breezes o'er it swept,
   A wanton zephyr broke the string.
And as its shriek died on the ear,
   (That chord's wild shriek when snapped in twain,)
With measured sounds 't was grief to hear,
   The musing maid prolonged the strain, —
"Oh thus, 't is thus with her who spreads
   Her bosom chords for Love to ring;
His breath inconstant breaks the threads,
   And leaves the heart a tuneless thing."

She bore a floweret from the shade,
   And raised it to the beams of day,
But while the light around it played,
   It withered 'neath the burning ray;
And as she marked each fragrant leaf
   Fast shrinking in the noon-day glare,
Again those mellowed tones of grief
   Stole soft along the scented air, —
"Oh thus, 't is thus with her, unwise,
   Who courts the sun of Passion's eye,
Mid lights that seemed of heavenly rise
   The startled dreamer wakes — to die."

COME THOU AT NIGHT.

Come thou at night, when soft through shadows
    gleaming,
  The fire-fly's lamp flits o'er the dusky lea,
Such is the light, oh thou of gentle dreaming,
  'Neath which to linger at the trysting-tree.

Chorus.

Yes, come at night, for then, 't is then, believe, love,
  I wait thy step, the sleeping flowers among;
The shadowy night, 't will not, 't will not deceive,
    love,
  It is the morn which hath a tell-tale tongue.

At break of morn Aurora will be peeping
  About thy lattice with her curious ray;
Ah, never trust a secret to her keeping,
  She only shines Love's blushes to betray.

Chorus.

But come at night, for then, 't is then, believe, love,
  I wait thy step, the sleeping flowers among;
The shadowy night, 't will not, 't will not deceive,
    love,
  It is the morn which hath a tell-tale tongue.

THE MANIAC'S VISION.

They say I'm mad, because I try
   With shouts to calm my brain;
And when I dance — I know not why —
   They bind me with a chain.
Avaunt! halloo! — I will be gay!
   Grief counts but little worth;
Since I have wept my tears away,
   What have I left but mirth?

Bring me companions! *am* I mad?
   No wonder I should rave —
They took the only one I had,
   And hid her in a grave;
And I'm kept *here* — a merry thing —
   Wherefore full well I know;
Ha! ha! because I laugh and sing,
   They will not let me go.

I saw the moon come down last night
   And dance upon the sea;
Go, catch her ere she takes to flight
   And bar her up with me.
The sun, they say, at rise of day,
   Did what he should not do;

He smiled, and made the hills look gay,
  And should be prisoned too.

And yonder star is quite as bad, —
  Run, seize it ere it fly;
We 'll dance together — *all are mad* —
  Sun, moon, and star, and I!
Look! ho! aside my fetters cast!
  That image, — loose my chain!
'T is she — she 's there — help! hold her fast!
  Ha! ha! she 's mine again.

FORT MILLER, *California*.

OH, BLAME HER NOT.

Oh, blame her not that she hath erred,
    Love made her vision dim,
See how the fount of tears is stirred!
    She weeps — and weeps for him.
The heart, once Nature's garden wild,
    Is now a desert spot,
Have pity on misfortune's child!
    Kind lady, blame her not.

Oh, blame her not, — 't is more than shame
    Love's robes to thus unfold,
Where hearts are made of lava flame,
    Who could expect them cold?
For her there is no kindred breath,
    Oh, be her guile forgot!
Her earthly doom is more than death, —
    Dear lady, blame her not.

Oh, blame her not, — despite the din
    Prude voices help to swell,
Her deepest fault, her darkest sin
    Was that she loved too well.
Devotion was her grand complaint,
    Desertion is her lot;
Her soul is sick, her heart is faint, —
    Sweet lady, blame her not.

SONNET TO THE OCEAN.

Dark dashing Ocean with thy crest of foam,
   Forever changing, and yet still the same,
How many wanderers o'er thy billows roam
   To seek for fortune or in quest of fame!
The widowed wife hath cursed thee — as she pressed
   The lips that ne'er may breathe a father's name;
And the fair bride, with tears and throbbing breast,
   Hath gazed upon thee from her silent home,
In mute despair, that thou should'st prove to be
   The grave of all she loved on earth the best.
Roll on, heave up thy waves in inward strife,
   Thou ever restless, ever sounding sea!
By yonder moon thou seemest bright — like life —
   But thou art fraught — like life — with treachery.

CHERISHED TOKENS.

I have a bird, a lovely bird,
   With saffron-colored wings,
And when the blessed morning breaks
   Ah me, how sweet he sings!
He perches on the window where
   It looks upon the sea,
And oh! his every note is soft
   As melody can be.

I have a tree, a scented tree,
   Brought from far Southern bowers,
And every month it bears for me
   A coronal of flowers.
Though fragile be that wreath it weaves,
   And soon its verdure past,
'T is sweet to watch the opening leaves,
   And love them while they last.

I have a lute, a deep-toned lute,
   With chords of rarest thrill,
And when at night the birds are mute,
   And winds and waves are still,
(Sometimes even by daylight's hour,)
   It sings or seems to sing

Such wild sad strains, I 've almost thought
  An angel touched its string.

I have a braid, a silken braid
  Of softest flaxen hair,
With clasp, which part of gold is made,
  And part a jewel rare;
They say the gold is thrice refined,
  And costlier far the gem,
And yet the simple lock they bind,
  I value more than them.

And I have, ah me, how little prized
  Of all my cherished things!
Hid in my bosom's deepest nook
  A heart of passion's strings.
I have, no, no! I have it not —
  It once was in that cell —
But now I fear 't is flown away, —
  Whither I may not tell.

CHIDE MILDLY THE ERRING.

Chide mildly the erring,
    Kind language endears,
Grief follows the sinful,
    Add not to their tears.
Avoid with reproval
    Fresh pain to bestow,
The heart that is stricken
    Needs never a blow.

Chide mildly the erring,
    Blame gently their fall,
If strength were but human,
    How weakly were all!
What marvel the pilgrim
    Should wander astray,
When tempests so shadow
    Life's wearisome way!

Chide mildly the erring,
    Rebuke them with care;
Compared with the *Perfect*,
    The best might despair.
We all have some failing,
    We all are unwise,
And the light which redeems us
    Must shine from the skies.

THE COTTAGE GIRL.

A voice from the chamber rang soft through the room:
"Sweet mother, relieve me from working the loom,
And up to the hill-side permit me to stray,
I'm weary with throwing the shuttle to-day.
There's a sound that I hear like the voice of a dream,
Which is sweet to my heart as I muse by the stream,
For something of late hath come over my breast,
That I love to look out on the clouds of the west;
The evening is mild and the sunset is fair,
And the bird, and the bee, and the Stranger are there."

A voice from the dairy continued the chime:
"Sweet mother, all day have I sorted the thyme,
My bosom is sick at the sound of the churn,
I cannot remain for the curdle to turn.
The dew-drops of labor stand moist on my brow,
The task was so wearisome milking the cow;
But fresh on the hill-side the apricot-tree,
And the rosy red currants are smiling for me,

While soft from the boughs hangs the mellow ripe
    pear,
And the peach, and the plum, and the Stranger are
    there."

I stood by the porch of the artless and poor;
But the sound of the shuttle came not from the
    door,
And hard by the threshold with moss overgrown
The herd unattended were feeding alone,
While a robin sang soft by the curb of the well,
Some tale, could it speak, as if anxious to tell.
And who was the mortal and where was he born
Who drew from the cottage the maid to the lawn?
Oh, ask me no further! but mothers take care
Of your blushing sixteen — should the Stranger
    come there.

    Hummock, *Okee-fee-nokee Swamp, Fla.*

THE DEATH OF MARY.

It is the hour thy evening hymn
    Was wont to soothe mine ear,
And silent in thy chamber dim
    I stand beside thy bier.
I gaze at yonder vacant chair,
    Then shuddering turn to thee;
Thou answer'st not my earnest stare,—
    Dear Mary, speak to me.

Ye placid lips give back your breath,
    Your smile still lingers here;
And thou, fair cheek, who says 't is death
    Maketh its hues so clear?
Thou art not dead — too rich the flush
    Along that purple vein —
'Tis roseate sleep which bids such blush,
    And thou wilt smile again.

Avaunt! ye phantoms of the cloud
    Which mock me for your mirth!
Avaunt, away, the winding shroud
    Was made for things of earth;
But thou did'st not to earth belong,
    Thy mansion was above;

Thou wert the Spirit of a song,
  Whose every note was love.

Beneath those orbs where seeming hid,
  The soul's bright flashes lie,
Still burns the lightning of the lid, —
  No, no, thou could'st not die!
Yet something, as I fix my gaze
  On those sealed orbs of sleep,
Strangely upon my bosom weighs,
  Prompting the wish to weep.

And one by one, as slowly start
  The herald drops of pain,
Something soft murmurs to my heart,
  That I have loved in vain;
That I must live without a ray
  On life's tempestuous sea,
To light the hope which pale decay
  Oh Mary, quenched with thee.

FORT GILMER, *January* 22*d*, 1839.

UNREQUITED LOVE.

There is a grief which all have known
Who ever mourned a friendship flown,
And few but what have shed the tear
Bewailing loss of token dear.
But ah! that grief is little cost
For friendship dead or token lost,
To hers whose lot it is to prove
The pang of unrequited love.
When after all that woman's art
Can do to curb that rebel heart,
The mask of smiles put on to veil
Her feelings as her cheek grows pale,
The courteous nod, the careless tone
Which seems to say she cares for none,
With every plea of maiden pride,
At length exhausted or defied,
She feels 't is idle to restrain
The throb which tells she loves in vain.

THE RETORT.

"Susie, playful child of Nature,
    Ever romping round the school,
How to kiss, you crazy creature,
    Can't you teach me, think, the rule?"

"Knowledge comes by pain and peril!
    Ain't it fun to teach a fool?"
O'er my lips she plied her ferule,—
    "Learn," said she, "to kiss by *rule*."*

    * An un-ruly retort.

SERENADE.

Wake, lady, wake! that gentle eye
   The voice of music bids unclose;
We stand beneath thy lattice high,
   To woo thee from thy soft repose;
The spell of sleep is scarce so strong,
   But wizard words the charm may break;
By the deep power of mighty song,
   We bid thee, wake! fair lady, wake!

Wake, lady, wake! upon the lea
   The stars look down serenely bright;
The moon hath fled beyond the sea,
   That thou may'st reign the queen of night;
Arouse! no cloud obscures the skies,
   No ripple stirs the tranquil lake,
Lift the fair lid which veils those eyes,
   Fair lady, wake! sweet lady, wake!

FIRST LOVE.

Though bards may sing — for love's regrets
    There is a stream oblivious flows,
Think not that woman's heart forgets
    The boon of faith it first bestows.
When pining o'er the leafless void
    Which life's romance hath failed to fill,
Regretting moments unemployed,
    She sighs for *something* dearer still;

If on the wing of thoughts that rove
    From soul to soul, from breast to breast,
She find at length — that wandering dove —
    A spot on which her heart may rest,
Say not, when passion's flood subsides,
    And life becomes a gentle stream,
She e'er forgets, along its tides,
    The olive of that early dream.

Though time and distance both should try
    To wring that vision from the past,
They cannot break the secret tie
    Which holds, spell-bound, its memory fast.
No, no, the God she thought divine
    May prove a shape of earthly care,
The light may vanish from the shrine —
    But still the pilgrim worships there.

HYMN FOR LILLA.

There is an angel in my way
    You cannot see.
So potent is her mystic sway,
That like a star of restless ray,
She haunts my path by night and day
    Where'er I be.

If she were woman I had known
    Her human birth;
Her look, her smile, her air alone,
The mortal's nature would have shown,
But there is something in her tone,
    Oh! not of earth.

Fair, radiant image! tell me why
    Thou roamest here,
Mid hearts that change and hopes that die!
Are there no denizens of sky
To worry with that troublous eye? —
    Back to thy sphere!

"THE WREATH YOU TWINED."

The wreath you twined at morn for me
    Faded before the eve grew dim;
The harp you hung in yonder tree
    Forgot as soon its wild-wood hymn;
To-morrow's sun, though bright he shine,
    Bloom to that wreath will not restore;
The breeze around that harp may pine,
    But ah! its strings will sound no more.

There was a time, in passion's bower,
    When, mid our dream of soft unrest,
To thee and me (oh, angel hour!)
    Came the fond thought — how *both* were blest.
Deceitful dream! when hope was high,
    And eyes gazed out on starlight bright,
That strewed with clouds love's summer sky,
    And veiled the heart in robes of night!

Oh! empty worship — such as mine —
    To sanctify a thing of earth,
To kneel before a human shrine,
    And find the idol little worth!
Fruit — rich, ripe fruit, whose juice to sip
    One would forego his heavenly share —
To press the apple to the lip,
    And have it turn to ashes there!

LIFE DREAMS.

All my life has been a dream,
Changeful as a moonlight gleam;
Now a shadow — now a beam
    O'er a desert cast;
Every color of the sky,
From the rainbow's deepest dye
To the azure of an eye
    Whose dear light is past.

Softly rising from afar,
Broad it shone, a dazzling star,
Till at length it grew a bar
    'Twixt myself and Heaven;
But the influence is gone,
And the shrine is left alone;
What its worshipers have done,
    Let it be forgiven.

Ever on my wandering way,
As from clouds at close of day,
Glides the pleasing sunset ray,
    So my visions fade;
Still dissolving with the hour,
Whether wreath from ivy bower,

Whether crown from throne of power,
    Or from sylvan maid.

Thankless work, this task of mine,
Lengthening still this silvery line,
When the fragile wire I twine
    Breaks at every turn!
Hapless bard, forbear thy strain!
Cast aside Love's shattered chain!
Thou may'st fan Hope's fire again —
    But no more 't will burn.

MEASURE FOR MUSIC.

WRITTEN IN ANSWER TO THE POPULAR LITTLE MELODY ENTITLED "CALL ME PET NAMES, DEAR."

Yes! I'll call thee pet names, dear,
  Mine only — my own,
My bud and my blossom,
  My kingdom — my throne.
I'll style thee a queen, dear,
  A goddess divine,
Whose heart is my temple,
  Whose brow is my shrine.

Yes! I'll give thee pet names, dear,
  My darling — my dove,
My joy and my jewel,
  My life and my love.
I'll seek for pet names, dear,
  'T is sweetest to call,
My bird and my bright one,
  My angel — my all.

LOVE AND THE LILY.

As Love one day was out at play,
   He met a blooming Lily,
And on its bosom asked to lay
   His cheek — it was so chilly.

"Go to," the wary Lily said,
   "I lack not for politeness;
But on my word, Love, I'm afraid
   Your cheek may soil my whiteness."

"Nay, nay, not so," Love soft replied,
   "You only talk for teazing;
'T is summer sunlight at your side,
   Else, everywhere, 't is freezing."

Believing not Love's seeming toil
   Was half he represented,
The pitying Lily all the while
   Refusing, still consented.

But when the morn with dewy tread
   Came round to wake the flowers,
Alas! the Lily's drooping head
   Rose not to greet the hours.

And though the bees around its cup
  At noon as usual dallied,
Oh, never more were lifted up
  The leaves which Love had sullied.

LINES TO E——.

Love thee? from the first moment when
    Thy fairy image blessed my sight,
On thee each thought by day hath been,
    On thee — still thee — each dream by night.
The warrior's love the world may know,
    'T is stamped with blood on flashing steel,
But who may tell or what may show
    The deep wild passion minstrels feel?

Love thee? go, ask the stars that keep
    Their midnight watch in yonder sky,
At the lone hour when others sleep,
    Whose was the ever-wakeful eye?
Go, tell the echoes to proclaim
    That slumber on yon mountain's crest,
Whose was the voice and what the name
    That waked them from their nightly rest.

Love thee? here gaze upon this brow,
    Which once they whispered me was fair,
All changed and flushed with fever now,
    What means the wasting token there?
This breast, whose throb no words can tell,
    This aching heart, this burning brain, —
These are thy answers, read them well,
    And never, never doubt again.

STANZAS.

TO THE FAIR POETESS OF MARIPOSA.

LADY of the gentle brow,
Breathing words of measured flow,
Sending soft a murmuring tone,
From the wilderness alone.
By the power of "runic rhymes,"
Hear and heed these mystic chimes!
Though by others all forgot,
Lady sweet, forget me not.

Fresno's rapids running soft
Bring to mind thy presence oft,
Calling back remembered hours,
Passed with thee mid Indian bowers;
Fresno lyrest, fair to see,
Thou art fled from stream and me;
Would'st thou wipe away the blot,
Lady sweet, forget me not.

By the lip of melting tone,
Breathing melody alone;
By the ringlet's jetty gleam
Mirrored in the Fresno stream,

By the form of fragile grace,
By thy thoughtful pensive face,
Telling tales — I scarce know what —
Lady sweet, forget me not.

By the light which o'er me burst
When I saw thy bright eye first,
By the shadow o'er me cast
When I saw that bright eye last,
By thy voice of soft farewell,
Saddening where its music fell,
By our sympathetic lot,
Lady sweet, forget me not.

FORT MILLER, *Mariposa Co., Cal.*

NEVER MORE.

Shall again her glance pursue me?
      Never more!
Shall her gentle words subdue me?
      Never more!
Faded is the wreath which crowned her,
Broken is the spell that bound her,
And my heart will sigh around her,
      Never more!

Shall again her lip caress me?
      Never more!
Shall her arms in fondness press me?
      Never more!
Ever since our last cold meeting,
In despair of kinder greeting,
Strangely I have kept repeating,
      Never more!

WHAT SHALL I TELL HER?

What shall I tell her? shall I say
    "O thou who art my throne,
At morn, at eve, for thee I pray,
    For thee I live alone?"
No, no! she'll mark my faltering mien,
    The truth she'll soon divine,
And she will say, "Another queen
    Is now already thine."

What shall I tell her? shall I trace
    The look I love to see,
And murmur, "Oh, for model grace,
    Pencil should paint but thee?"
No, no! she'll tell, amid her tears,
    Of Time's effacing dye,
How canvas soon is changed with years,
    And cast neglected by.

What shall I tell her? shall I look
    Into her eyes of blue,
And whisper, "O, thou radiant book,
    I read from only you?"
No, no! she'll state how man deceives,
    Treats light such books of store,

How heedless fingers soil the leaves,
  Or turn them idly o'er.

What shall I tell her? not a word
  These cold, calm lips shall say;
Within my bosom, like a sword,
  Close sheathed my voice shall lay.
In the dark cavern of my breast,
  Like shell in Ocean's cave,
The thought there born there too shall rest, —
  Love's " cradle, and his grave."

TWILIGHT STANZAS.

As dim the veil of evening spread,
Where blushed the clouds with sunset red,
A passion youth, by love opprest,
Sang as he watched the golden west: —

    "Thou bird with buzzing wing that flies
        All day among the flowers,
    Go, tell the maid with soft blue eyes,
        'T is thus *she* haunts my hours."

As fainter now, and fainter still,
The hues of daylight tinged the hill,
Again from passion's melting tongue
Of her he loved the music rung: —

    "Ye shadows length'ning to repose,
        Along the sunset streams,
    Go, tell the maid with cheek of rose,
        She darkens thus my dreams."

BEAUTY SLEEPING.

She slept! along her arm of snow
   Her cheek of rose serene was laid,
While clustering curls heaved to and fro
   On every wave her breathings made.
Each zephyr, as it stole along,
   Went past her couch with lighter air,
As loath to wake, with pinion strong,
   The thing of joy which slumbered there.

She slept! the thin, transparent lid
   Curved calmly o'er her eye of blue,
But though the earthly orb was hid,
   The spirit light still struggled through,
While o'er her lip alternate wrought
   A quivering pulse which went and came,
As if some dream renewed the thought,
   The waking hours had ceased to name.

She slept! and as the moonlight rays
   Streamed down and kissed her forehead pale,
(Sly rovers! little loath to gaze
   On charms which night forgets to veil,)
'T was marvel not why things of air,
   Bright shapes which once in heaven had shone,
Attracted by a sight so fair,
   For woman's home should leave their own.

AND THOU WERT FALSE.

"*La jalousie suit de près l'amour.*"

And thou wert false — so let it be!
   If o'er that shrine of beauty rare,
There bends unchecked the stranger's knee,
   The stranger's heart may worship there.

A chain was wove, a spell was cast, —
   The links are broke, the charm is free,
And Memory, when she views the past,
   Must skip the page which tells of thee.

I little thought, when o'er thy heart
   My spirit poised her raptured wings,
And trembling tried, with guileless art,
   To wake the music of its strings,

That every chord where passion slept
   An echo gave of heedless swell,
That every string the angel swept,
   Another's touch might wake as well:

That like the lyre which hangs alone
   Where summer winds are wont to play,

To every breeze 't would yield a tone,
    For every ear 't would breathe a lay.

Forget'st thou in that lonely bower,
    Which drooping myrtles clustered o'er,
The pledge we gave, of glowing power,
    In token of the vow we swore?

When o'er thy yielding form I hung,
    And craved it for my spirit's shrine.
And gathered from thy murm'ring tongue
    The low response which sealed thee mine?

And thou wert false! so let it be;
    If o'er that shrine of beauty rare,
There bends unchecked the stranger's knee,
    The stranger's heart may worship there.

CAUTION.

EXTRACT FROM AN EARLY POEM.

.... Trust ever doubtingly!
I tell thee, Lilla, friendship is a name
By which fond hearts are covertly betrayed.
Falsehood and faith meander side by side,
Like neighboring streams which meet and mix in one.
     Hopes are like bubbles
That burst when biggest, and a lover's vow
Is like the dew which at Aurora's smile
Melts into nothingness.
     Love chains the soul
As opiates bind the senses — 't is not sleep —
'T is but a trance which doth resemble sleep,
A deep unrest of strangely mingled dreams,
From which the fevered sufferer wakes to mourn,
Vainly, o'er memories perished.

ALEIDA.

Thou hast passed from my heart like the dew from the spray,
Like the bloom from the bud, like the light from the day.
Oh, sad is the shade which thy memories leave
As the cloud which hangs dark on the brow of the eve!
The gleam has gone out from those beautiful eyes
Like a star which has set never more to arise.
And the rays of fond Hope which once glistened in mine
Are mingled and lost in the twilight with thine.

Aleida! Aleida! stray lamb of the fold!
There's a tale of the fleece which 't is hard to be told,
A story, low whispered, of evil and thee,
Which uncontradicted, oh, never should be!
By the rose of that cheek which I've trembled to touch,
By the snow of that brow which I've lauded so much,
By thine eye's earnest gaze and thy lip's gentle tone,
Aleida! Aleida! come back to thine own.

Come back to the home of thy innocent mirth,
Where thy mother sits sad by the desolate hearth,
And thy silver-haired father, the winter eve long,
Impatiently yearns for thy accents of song.
Return, thou estranged one, restore us thy smile,
And thy rosy cheek brother shall greet thee the while;
Return to thy sister — *she* cannot forget —
She loves her Aleida — she worships her yet.

Aleida! thou mother — yet never a bride!
I speak not to chide thee — 't were idle to chide, —
Do I weep? 'T is not weakness! strength wrestles in vain
When the fount overflows with the dew-drops of pain.
Tears? Yes! — nor expect me the torrent to stay, —
When the flood-gates are lifted the stream must have way.
Oh! grief, — how I loved thee, words never may tell!
Aleida, Aleida! farewell — fare thee well.

SOFTLY THE SENTRY STARS OF NIGHT

Softly the sentry stars of night
  Shine down, my love, on thee,
And I am jealous of the sight,
  Uncalled, they share with me.

I do not sigh for shining gold,
  I do not pine for gear,
All that on earth I care to hold
  Lies softly pillowed here.

This Parian brow like marble fair,
  This cheek of palest rose,
These breathing lips of carmine rare,
  Oh! more than wealth compose.

I watch thy sleeping brow above,
  Wake, dearest, I am thine;
Lift thy fringed lids, my dreaming love,
  And whisper, "Thou art mine."

I WILL NOT LEAVE THEE NOW.

I will not leave thee to the scorn
    Of colder hearts than thine,
The cloud which veils thy sunny morn
    Hath also darkened mine.
Though worldlings whisper that the stain
    Of sin is on thy brow,
Warping alike thy heart and brain,
    I will not leave thee now.

I know that some will meet thine eye
    With look of curious gaze,
While some will coldly pass thee by,
    Who once would stop to praise.
And yet of these — or yet of them,
    Who first the stone will throw?
They err the most who most condemn, —
    I will not leave thee now.

No, I'll not slight thee! what is done
    Perhaps may not endure;
I'll only think of thee as one
    Who once was bright and pure.
Thy youth, thy bloom, thy trusting heart,
    Thy fair confiding brow, —
'T was these which made thee what thou art:
    I will not leave thee now.

I EVER DREAM OF THEE.

I DREAM of thee, my Mary own,
    When near and far away;
When stars are on their midnight throne,
    And in the noon of day;
Thy gentle image from my heart,
    Whatever change may be,
Nor time may change, nor distance part, —
    I ever dream of thee.

I dream of thee when Autumn rings
    The death-dirge of the flowers;
When Spring returns on dewy wings,
    To woo the laughing hours.
Though Winter weave his fleecy chain
    Along the frozen lea,
Or smiling Summer deck the plain,
    I ever dream of thee.

I dream of thee when sickness strews
    My couch with thorns of pain,
Still, still of thee when health renews
    My bounding pulse again;
Alike in chambers sad and lone,
    As in the halls of glee,
I dream of thee, my Mary own,
    I ever dream of thee.

THE UNREGRETTED.

She has passed away — she has passed away,
    And not a tear is shed;
Not a sob is heard, as the prayers they say
    Over the voiceless dead.
Night with its stars availed her not,
    And nothing the gorgeous day,
Hers upon earth was a lonely lot, —
    But away — she has passed away.

A brow of pain and a hand of toil,
    And limbs that failed at need,
And a heart that shrank at the world's turmoil,
    These were her daily meed.
Wishing for night with its restless sleep,
    Longing for morning's ray,
Hers was the task to watch and weep, —
    But away — she has passed away.

She has winged her flight to the heavenly gates
    Where the "King of Glory" stands,
To the chamber where the "Bridegroom waits,"
    To the "house not made with hands."
On the shining shore her lot is cast,
    Where "living fountains" play;
Home, home, oh joy! to her *home* at last, —
    Away — she has passed away.

MARY'S LIPS ARE RED WITH ROSES.

(ANACREONTIC.)

Mary's lips are red with roses,
   Yet how cold the words they say!
Joy on Mary's cheek reposes,
   Yet that cheek is turned away;
Still for all this careless seeming,
Mary's eye serenely beaming,
Shines like starlight through my dreaming,
           Night and day.

Mary's lips may learn their folly,
   When the hour is past for bliss;
And her cheek of melancholy
   Vainly turns in search of this;
When she finds how humors vary,
Then perhaps may *frugal* Mary
Mourn the hour she was so chary
           Of a kiss.

LATTICE PEEPING.

Butterfly, butterfly! minion of light,
Floating like gossamer fast from my sight!
Tell me — come, whisper ere further you rove,
Have ye met as ye journeyed the smile of my love?
" Whoever thy mistress, she stood not, I ween,
This morn as I passed at her lattice of green,
For I peeped at each crevice, but nought could I see
Save the fair mignonette and the sweet-scented pea."

Humming-bird, humming-bird! gentlest of wing,
Sipping the sweets from each delicate thing!
Say, ere ye sail to your nest in the grove,
Have ye heard at her lattice the voice of my love?
"That I've peeped at each casement the morning
    breeze knows,
For it bent to my kisses the tulip and rose,
But nought have I heard at the porch of thy fair,
Save the buzz of the bee as he whizzed through
    the air."

Butterfly, butterfly! fading in blue!
Humming-bird, humming-bird! sipping the dew!
Bring ye no word of my mistress to-day?
Swift o'er the hill to yon cottage away!

There where the peony and princes' red plume
'Neath her soft culture have blushed into bloom,
Hover around her and flutter above,
Till ye catch at her lattice a peep of my love.

THINK NOT THAT I LOVE THEE.

Think not that I love thee!
　　Ah! how may it be?
In the hush of the twilight,
　　I think not of thee;
And the voice of my lute-string,
　　As it floats o'er the frame,
Mid all its soft murmurs,
　　Breathes never thy name.

Think not that I love thee!
　　'T were an idle surmise, —
Love lives in the accents,
　　Love dwells in the eyes;
And never by glances,
　　And never by tone,
Has thy bosom discovered
　　One thought of my own.

Think not that I love thee!
　　No story I tell,
Can woman dissemble
　　So wise and so well?
Then go, and forget me,
　　'T is vain to repine,
For my heart, though 't were breaking,
　　Can never be thine.

WHY DOTH MUSIC CHARM NO MORE?

I.

Why doth music charm no more?
  'T is because thy smile has faded;
Why hath life but little store?
  'T is that thou its joy hast shaded.
    Hope hath lost her cherished token,
    Love bewails a lute-string broken,
    Words thy lips should *not* have spoken,
      Memory weepeth o'er.

II.

Time there was I prized thee well!
  Ask ye why the charm is over?
Words there are full plain will tell:
  "*Roving heart — inconstant lover.*"
    Myrtle-wreath is changed for willow —
    Bark of Love is wrecked by billow —
    O'er that bosom once his pillow —
      Toll the funeral-knell.

THE UNREQUITED.

He left her in her beauty's pride
  Sadly to sit alone,
He who had worshiped at her side
  And trembled at her tone!
They met in halls of glittering light,
  But not as once before —
Although her lip smiled *very* bright —
  It smiled for *him* no more.

He left her, and with phrases fair
  Unto another turned,
While yet was trembling on the air
  The words for *him* that burned;
He came once more with accents dear
  And craved that slighted strain —
But ah! the songs he loved to hear
  She never breathed again.

He left her, as the fickle wind
  Leaves flowers that scent the lea.
While every word bore welcome kind,
  And look as love's should be;
But when, upon her face to gaze,
  He came a later day,

The eye, whose glance he loved to praise,
   Was coldly turned away.

He left her to the cold applause
   Of flatterers smiling gay,
He said, he scarcely knew the cause,
   Yet still he stayed away.
Time may perhaps again restore
   Her image to his brain,
But he has lost what never more
   Shall beat for him again.

THE GRAVE OF MELLON.

[ON the desolate shore of Lake Monroe, in Florida, there is a grave overshadowed by a solitary cypress. This tree, probably from its isolated position, had become the resort of a whippoorwill, whose mournful notes, on a still night, could be distinctly heard by the troops of the United States garrison stationed in the vicinity. The grave is that of the ill-fated Mellon who perished, at an early period of the Florida War, during an attack of the Seminole Indians upon the fort which bears his name.]

WHY seek this lonely ground,
   Thou melancholy bird?
Why o'er this little grassy mound,
When evening's shadows gather round,
   Are thy sad accents heard?

Know'st thou yon cypress limb
   Shadeth the couch of death?
Yet there, thick-veiled mid shadows dim,
All night thou pour'st thy funeral hymn
   Along the deep wind's breath.

Is it the chiming roar
   Of waves that come and go?
Is it the night-wind moaning o'er
What tears may ne'er again restore,
   That binds thy soul to woe?

Hath not the day-star power
  To urge thee into song, —
Day, which brings gladness to the bower,
Lifting the lids of the sleeping flower, —
  Day, with its sunlight strong?

Sing when the mock-bird sings!
  When the locust and the bee
Blend their low melody of wings
With the glad strains which morning brings!
  Oh, why is night for thee?

Ah! bird to sadness dear,
  'T is thine to pour the wail
O'er one thou lov'st to linger near,
All plaintive to the starlight clear
  Repeating still the tale.

Yes, thine it is to tell,
  With ever-constant tone,
How he who braved the charge so well,
Neath the same spot on which he fell,
  Sleeps silent, cold, and lone.

FORT MELLON, *Florida*, *May*, 1842.

THE BRIDE'S DEPARTURE.

Brother! speak in whispers light,
'T is my last — my last good-night!
Never more our steps will stray
Through the garden's scented way;
By the homestead of the bees,
'Neath the shady chesnut-trees;
By the meadow's winding stream,
Glittering in the sunset beam;
Gentle brother, smile and bless —
'T is my last — my last caress.

Sister! with thine eyes of blue,
Hither come and weep "adieu!"
Let thy arm around me twine,
Let thy cheek repose on mine,
While I gaze into thy face
Circled in this dear embrace!
Thou hast ever proved to me
All that love could wish to be;
Yet I leave thy heart alone, —
Brother! sister! bless your own.

Mother! thou hast rocked my head
Softly on its cradle bed;

When the storm was raging high
Sweetly sung love's lullaby;
Yet I part, I part from *thee*, —
Who, henceforth, will sing to me?
When my forehead aches with pain
I shall miss that early strain.
Mother! with thy accents mild,
Once more bless thy weeping child.

Father, thou hast loved me well, —
More than human tongue may tell;
More than wealth, from childhood's hour,
Thou hast lavished on thy flower;
Now thy locks are waxing gray,
From thy heart I pass away.
Never more thy lips at eve
On my cheek their kiss will leave;
In the prayer of undertone,
Mother! father! bless your own.

THE PASSING BELL.*

" Dust to dust — ashes to ashes."

"Dust to dust," yon solemn bell
   Daily says or seems to say;
Hark! its rolling, tolling knell, —
   "Dust to dust and clay to clay."
By the angel now at rest,
   By the flower my bosom wore,
(Snatched untimely from my breast,)
   Hollow herald, toll no more!

Hast thou, tongue of iron frame,
   Never note for larum call,
Tone to tell of threat'ning flame,
   Joyous sound for festive hall?
Yonder moves the bridal train, —
   Peal love's merry roundelay!
Tolls the deep bell back again,
   "Dust to dust and clay to clay."

"Dust to dust" — once more that sound
   Thrills upon the listening ear;

---

* Suggested by the frequent tolling of the bell at Trinity Church, at Newport, R. I., during the prevalence of a severe epidemic.

Under-voices whisper round,
  Tearful glances watch the bier!
Like as billows fall and rise,
  Echo answers far away —
(Bridegroom, turn aside your eyes) —
  " Dust to dust and clay to clay."

Whose is now the requiem lone
  Pealing on the evening wind?
Whose is now the spirit gone,
  Leaving hearts of care behind?
Tolling from the belfry high,
  'Neath the hammer's measured play,
Slowly surged that one reply, —
  " Dust to dust and clay to clay."

THE RELEASED SPIRIT.

"By the garland on the bier
Weep, a maiden claims thy tear."
MRS. HEMANS.

SISTER, wild with many a prank,
Romping o'er the violet-bank,
Till afar like misty screen
Sky and dim wood intervene!
She who twined amid thy hair
Flowers 't was thy delight to wear;
She hath bid farewell to thee, —
Sister, weep and bend the knee.

Brother, with thy brow of dread
Bronzed on fields where warriors tread,
And thy tone of stern command,
Thrilling mid our household band,
And thy look of marksman pride!
Come and view the *archer's* bride;
Silent is her voice of glee, —
Brother, weep and bend the knee.

Mother, with thy heart unstrung,
Grieving for the fair and young,
From thy wilderness of grief,
Vainly pleading for relief!

Come, where sorrow hath no thrill,
Where the moan of pain is still:
Here, beside the precious clay,
Weeping mother, come and pray.

Father, but on earth no more,
Thou, who ripe for heaven before,
Left *her* spirit bound in clay,
Panting for its bridal day!
From thy mansion in the skies,
Come, and help an angel rise;
See her smile of radiance mild, —
Father, Spirit, take thy child!

PRAYER OF THE YOUNG NOVICE.

Jesus, Prince of mystic birth,
King in heaven and man on earth,
One or Three — whiche'er thou art —
Son of Mary, shield my heart!

Where the censor's cloud ascends,
Sick at heart Thy handmaid bends,
If avail a maiden's tear,
Smile on her who worships here!

Pardon grant for what I tell;
I have loved — alas, too well;
That sweet idol *Thou* should'st be,
One on earth has been to me.

Yet when matins call to meet,
Here I come to kiss Thy feet;
Gazing on Thy image dim,
Here I pray at vesper hymn.

Oh, from out Thy rainbow crown,
Pour Thy mild effulgence down!
Shield me from this wild distress;
Son of Mary, smile and bless!

BRIDE, UPON THY MARRIAGE DAY.

LINES WRITTEN IN ACKNOWLEDGMENT OF A ROSE RECEIVED FROM THE HANDS OF A LADY ON THE EVE OF HER MARRIAGE.

Bride, upon thy marriage day,
Yielding all thy wealth away,
Wealth, thy lover would not bart,—
In the simple boon, thy heart!
By the pledge of rosy hue,
Softly passed to me from you,
Pray that He who *made* the flowers,
Guard thee when no longer "ours."

Soon with spell of golden band,
Will the ring be on thy hand;
Soon before the face of Heaven,
Will thy plighted vows be given.
But though passing sweet to be
With the one who lives for thee —
Never, mid thy altered lot,
Be thy parents' love forgot.

Bride, upon thy marriage eve,
Looking smiles, yet taking leave,
Casting off the ties at home,
By another's side to roam!

Pray, though joy its sense may dim,
Still thy soul may cling to *Him;*
From the safe and narrow way,
That thy footsteps never stray.

Ask that He who rules above
Teach thee from His book of love,
That His frown, in after years,
May not turn thy smiles to tears,
But through grace for thee and thine,
Ever more His mercy shine.
Bride, upon thy marriage day,
Wreathed with roses, kneel and pray!

SUNBEAMS AND SHADOWS.

> "All that's bright must fade,
> The brightest still the fleetest."

When the sky wears richest shade,
Then the sun begins to fade;
When the rose is fullest spread,
Then begins to droop its head.

Sweetest strains the song-birds sing,
At the hour they take to wing;
Softest is the rainbow's light,
At the time it fades from sight.

Morning's dew-drops shine most fair
Just before exhaled in air;
Evening's star-queen twinkles best,
Shortly ere it sinks to rest.

Such, ah such is human life! —
Peace, the harbinger of strife,
Smiles, forerunner of the tear,
Joy, but Sorrow's pioneer.

But there is a clime above,
Lighted by the sun of love,

Where the spirit free may range,
Unrepressed by earthly change;

Where Hope's smile will not deceive,
Pleasure leave the heart to grieve;
May our souls the grace be given,
To secure that changeless heaven!

FLOWERS AND POETRY FOR ADA.

" Bring flowers, fresh flowers for the fair young bride."
MRS. HEMANS.

DEAR Ada, keep these wild-flowers few
A father's hand has plucked for you;
Receive them as a pledge sincere
That father loves his daughter dear.
One is a flower vermillion dyed,
Soft symbol of a blushing bride;
Another white — an emblem sure
Of gentleness and virtue pure;
The third, an earnest still of you,
Is tinged with true love's loveliest blue.
Would, daughter dear, that I with this,
Could also send a parent's kiss.
But ocean rolls between us wild, —
A father's blessing on his child!

FORT MILLER, *California, March* 14, 1853.

THE AGED MOTHER.

[ALL day long she sits in her easy-chair, and dreams at night of her *little* children; pleasant dreams of youthful happiness which she will again realize in that country where the inhabitants shall never say " I am weary."] — *Epistle from a Sister.*

Oh, rouse her not — she sleeps —
   See how serene she lays!
Close by her chair an angel keeps!
   She dreams of earlier days.

The agony and strife,
   Of years twice two the score,
The passion and the *pride* of life, —
   Oh joy, she feels no more.

Unconscious of the hours
   Which flit life's sands away,
Her spirit roams mid birds and flowers
   Of girlhood's laughing day.

She sees the festive heel
   In the red lamp-light glance,
And threads again the faultless reel
   Of the good New England dance.

Around the homestead fire,
   (Whose light long since has gone,)

The young wife sits with child and sire,
    And feels no more alone.

Along the China tile *
    She shows each group of grace,
While feeble fingers strive, the while,
    To grasp the checkered face.

For them the board is set,
    For them the feast is spread,
They meet again as once they met,
    The *living* and the *dead*.

In memory's chamber dim
    She hears the wonted prayer,
She sings again the cradle-hymn,
    And thinks her offspring there.

And holier far than song,
    She hears the Sabbath chimes,
While slow her footsteps steal along
    The aisle of olden times.

She sleeps, behold her face!
    What smile of radiance rare!
Tread softly — 't is a holy place —
    An angel guards her chair.

---

* Alluding to the tiles by which the exterior of the old-fashioned fire-places was bordered. They were made of porcelain and decorated with Chinese figures, whose grotesque appearance was well calculated to excite the admiration of the "*young idea*."

LINES AT MY SISTER'S GRAVE.

Beside thy dewy grave I pass,
  (A fresh and flowery mound,)
Sunlight is glancing on the grass,
  And the redbreast chirps around;
While from afar the city's hum
  Steals gently on the ear;
And yet for me is Nature dumb, —
  Thy voice I cannot hear.

Thou told'st me, from a distant land,
  I ne'er should be forgot, —
I come — e'en at thy side I stand,
  And yet thou heed'st me not.
Where are those accents which were heard
  So oft on music's breath?
Sister! — I hear no answering word!
  Ah, say, can this be death?

Beside my father's aged form
  They've laid thee, breast to breast,
Too bitter was the world's bleak storm,
  But both are now at rest.
In life united — oh with such
  Affection undefiled!

In death 'tis well their coffins touch, —
   The father and the child.

Thou, sister, had'st but little strength
   To tread life's thorny track;
So calmly dost thou sleep at length,
   'T were sin to wish thee back;
The music of thy gentle tone
   Though to my bosom dear,
And though my heart is sad and lone,
   I would not have thee here.

For me is still life's stirring tide,
   The battle and the storm,
The wave where warring navies ride,
   The field where squadrons form;
But thou, with no long watch to keep,
   No dream at morn to tell, —
Freed one! thine is an envied sleep, —
   Sweet sister, fare thee well!

September 17, 1848.

DEATH OF ADA.

She sleeps! be still, my heart,
  Thy throbs are all in vain!
They cannot heal grief's bitter smart,
Nor all these blinding tears that start
  Recall her back again.

Why did she pass away
  And leave the sunlight here?
Why in yon chamber silent lay,
When close below were flowerets gay,
  And birds with songs of cheer?

Had not the goldfinch powers
  To stay her lapsing breath?
Music, whose magic chains the hours,
Perfumes, that feed the drooping flowers, —
  Were these in vain 'gainst death?

Then too should Love have died,
  And all Love holds in store, —
Alike the home of hearts allied,
And the sweet name of earthly bride
  Alike — for evermore!

Ada in climates mild
  There first I sang of thee!
Companion — friend through forests wild —
Wife — mother — daughter — cherished child —
  And is it *thou* I see?

Stiff folded — *frosty* fair
  Is this *thy* small white hand?
And these the locks of flaxen hair
Which floated on the sultry air
  In the far Southern land?

I bend above thy cheek,
  I stoop and kiss thy brow;
A father's lips, all quivering, seek
That forehead once so warm and meek,
  But cold as marble now.

Hid are those eyes of blue
  Within a *curtained* spot;
Yet on the lips I loved to view
Seems the same smile which once I knew,
  Save that *it changes not*.

One answering look of thine,
  And I would not complain!
One motion more from that cold shrine,
And I, methinks, would not repine
  Nor shed a tear again!

Could'st thou but wake to weep, —
One last sad word to tell!
But no, so calm thy slumber deep,
'T were cruel to disturb such sleep, —
Sweet daughter, fare thee well!

I'M STANDING BY THEE, FATHER DEAR.

I'm standing by thee, father dear,
  I'm standing close by thee;
And yet thy voice I do not hear,
  Thy face I do not see.
And, oh! I mourn with vain regret
  The smile of welcome mild,
Which ever greeted, when we met,
  Till *now*, thy wandering child.

I little thought when on that day,
  Dim with the mist of years,
Thou watched'st the bark which bore away
  The object of thy tears,
Although thy locks were frosted o'er
  By Time's ensilvering tide,
I ne'er again should see thee more,
  My parent and my guide.

A weary march I've had since then
  Over the world's wide plain;
I've wrestled in the strife with men,
  And battled with the brain;
By fortune prompted still to roam,
  I've ranged from land to land,

Now o'er the ocean's billowing foam,
  Now o'er the desert's sand.

And after many a month, my friend,
  And after many a year,
I come to bow where thou did'st bend,
  And I behold thy bier;
I reach once more the cherished spot,
  For which so long I've sighed,
Only to feel that thou art not,—
  Kind sire, that thou hast died.

NEWPORT, R. I., *September*, 1850.

THE PAST.

The past! the past! 't is all my dower,
   For that I live alone!
To sit, from morn till evening hour,
   And dream on what is gone.
And as through memory's shadowy glass
   My clouded sight I strain,
Dim images of youth-time pass
   Before my eyes again.

The parent forms so much I loved
   I see beside the hearth,
And where my little sisters roved,
   I hear the laugh of mirth.
And from the window where the sun
   Shone at the rise of day,
The garden flowers I look upon
   In the sweet month of May.

I see the time-piece where it stands
   In the old oaken hall,
And watch the movement of the hands,
   As round the face they crawl;
They always went so slow to me,
   I would have whipt them by,

Thinking, amid my childish glee,
   Time should be made to fly.

They tell me now my sire is dead,
   And that my home is changed,
That brothers — sisters — all have fled —
   Since I abroad have ranged.
This tale I count as most untrue,
   And one they must not name,
For oft I see, in fancy's view,
   That homestead still the same.

And if our house *is* turned around,
   It is not turned for me,
Full well I know the garden ground,
   And every bush can see.
And if abroad the words be told,
   One parent lives to grieve,
While one is sleeping 'neath the mould —
   The tale I'll not believe.

My brother's features too I see,
   And, beaming like a sun,
My sisters' eyes look round on me —
   My sisters, all but one —
She changed — *she* died — her heart was flame,
   And was too warm to last!
Save this — our home is still the same;
   I live but in the past.

INDIAN MELODIES.

"He sees his God in clouds, and hears him in the wind." — *Pope.*

THE SEMINOLE'S REPLY.

["THE attack on Fort Mellon, River St. Johns, Florida, was made, it is supposed, by 'Philip' and his gang. This action must have taken place before information of the truce was received by the Indians."] — *Southern paper*.

BLAZE, with your serried columns!
   I will not bend the knee!
The shackle ne'er again shall bind
   The arm which *now* is free.
I've mailed it with the thunder,
   Where the tempest muttered low,
And where it falls ye well may heed
   The lightning of the blow.

I've scared ye in the city,
   I've scalped ye on the plain —
Go seek your chosen where they fell
   Beneath my leaden rain.*
I scorn your proffered treaty —
   The pale-face I defy —

---

* At Dade's Massacre, which took place near Tampa Bay, Florida, in December 1835, the entire command, consisting of three companies of the United States Artillery, was slaughtered, with the exception of three individuals who escaped by feigning death during the progress of the work of destruction.

Revenge is stamped upon my spear
  And " *Blood* " my battle-cry.

Some strike for hope of booty,
  Some to defend their all —
I battle for the joy I have
  To see the white man fall.
I love, among the wounded,
  To hear his dying moan;
And catch, while chanting at his side,
  The music of his groan.

Ye 've trailed me through the forest!
  Ye 've tracked me o'er the stream!
And struggling through the everglade,
  Your bristling bayonets gleam;
But I stand as should the warrior,
  With his rifle and his spear,
The scalp of vengeance still is red —
  And warns ye — " *Come not here.*"

Think ye to find my homestead?
  I gave it to the fire!
My tawny household do ye seek?
  I am a childless sire! *
But should ye crave life's sustenance,
  Enough I have, and good;

---

* It will be remembered that many of the Seminoles destroyed their own children, they being considered an incumbrance to the war.

I live on hate — 't is all my bread,
   And light is not my food.

I loathe ye with my bosom,
   I scorn ye with mine eye,
And I 'll taunt ye with my latest breath
   And fight ye till I die.
I ne'er will ask ye quarter,
   And I ne'er will be your slave,
But I 'll swim the sea of slaughter,
   Till I sink beneath its wave.

"TA-BISE-QUONGH."*

[Upon the bank of a beautiful stream which empties itself into the Saint Clair, an Indian, by the name of Ta-bise-quongh, was one day discovered by an officer of the United States Army. His canoe was drawn up beside him on the sand and he was surrounded by a small but faithful remnant of his once-numerous followers. This chief was dying, and before the officer left the spot the " Voice of the Rolling Thunder " was hushed in the forest.]

Hunter, why thy bow unbent,
E'er the deadly shaft be sent?
Droops thy lofty spirit here,
On the ridge where haunt the deer?
Otters bask beneath the moon,
Boundeth by the fierce raccoon,
Traps are set, and scents are keen; —
Need-je! ka-win, Nee-shee-sheen.†

Brother, here are herbs for thee,
Plucked beside the sugar-tree;‡
Charmèd plants which only grow
In the groves of Manito;
Eat, and thou again shalt pass,
Swiftly through the tangled grass;
On my hand thy forehead lean, —
Need-je! ka-win, Nee-shee-sheen.

* Ta-bise-quongh or " Voice of the Rolling Thunder."
† Friend or brother, it is not well.
‡ Sugar-maple.

Hunter, lead the royal race,
Guide thy eagles to the chase!
Show thine arrow's glittering tongue,
Let the bear outstrip her young!
Raise thine arm of swarthy stain,
Let the wolf recoil again!
Was this not thy wonted mien?
Need-je! ka-win, Nee-shee-sheen.

Brother, raise thy drooping head,
'T is not here for royal bed;
Brother, lift the shaded eye,
This is not where princes lie.
Tell me, brother, is it thine —
Scattered leaf and fallen pine,
Thou with beads of blue and green?*
Need-je! ka-win, Nee-shee-sheen.

Hunter, hark! o'er forest dim
Bursts afar the thunder hymn;
Thunder Spirits muttering say,
" Rolling Brother, haste away!"
Need-je, need-je! thou shalt go
Where they bend the golden bow,
Where the fields are ever green, —
Need-je, need-je! Nee-shee-sheen.†

* Diversity of color, together with the quantity of beads worn by the Indian warrior, is supposed to indicate superiority of rank.
† Friend or brother, it is now well.

PAWNEE LOVE-SONG.

Sighing Swan of Wacomee,
Hear the words of Nepowee!
I have crushed the "Eagle's Claw,"
I have coped with Wabershaw,
But I come with words to thee,
Sweeter than the sugar-tree.
Sister to the "Sailing Dove,"*
Listen to my lay of love!

Daughter of the "Blazing Knife,"
I have saved thee in the strife,
Chased the wily "Fox" away
When Wacondah bid him slay;
I have sent the "Rushing Roe"
To the grove of Manito.
By the token scalp I bring,
Listen to the "Raven Wing!"

* *Sister to the Sailing Dove.* For the information of the uninitiated it may not be deemed inappropriate to state that the above words, marked as quoted, together with others of a similar character, are translations of terms which, in the original vernacular, are used by the aborigines to express tribal names. However euphonious they may sound to the ear of the native, the task would be a hopeless one to attempt embodying them within the confined limits of metrical composition.

Thou art graceful in thy pride,
As the swan on Kansa's tide,
Thou art lovely in thy might,
As the moon on Ozark's height,
Gently do thy accents flow,
As the stream of Wulwanow.
Smiling child of " Dawning Day,"
Listen to the hunter's lay!

I am mighty, I am strong,
I am son to *Ta-bise-quongh;*
Broken is the battle-charm
When I raise my thunder-arm;
Harmless steel and rageless fire
When I name my " Rolling Sire."
I am mighty — thou art mild —
Listen to the cloud-born child!

PAWNEE CURSE.

Spirit, rider of the air,
Listen to the red man's prayer!
Blight the "Long Knife"* with thy wrath;
Let the foeman haunt his path;
When he toils mid tangled brake,
Let him tread on poisoned snake;
When he stoops o'er gushing spring,
Let him taste the adder's sting;
When he shivers 'neath the storm,
Clothe him not with blanket warm.

Spirit, rider of the air,
Listen to the red man's prayer!
Let the pale-face thread the plain,
Ever doomed to hunt in vain;
May no deer at twilight dim
Raise the antlered head for him;
When the trout is in the brook,
May the line have lost its hook;
When he sees the startled hind,
May his hand no arrow find.

* *Long Knife.* A title used to designate a chief among the pale-faces.

Spirit, rider of the air,
Listen to the red man's prayer!
O'er the prairie's burning sea
Let the "Long Knife" hunted be;
When he flies his scorching bed,
Let his trail be marked with red;
Let him roam where forests scowl,
Startled by the panther's howl;
If he pause by spreading oak,
Blast him with the thunder-stroke.

Spirit, rider of the air!
Listen to the red man's prayer!
When the "Long Knife's" eye is dim
May no dirge be sung for him;
May that land he never know,
Where the tawny hunters go;
May no flag beside him wave;*
May no bark protect his grave;
Let no mother rend with sighs
Wigwam where the pale-face dies;
Spirit, rider of the air,
Listen to the red man's prayer!

* Among some of the tribes, it is customary to adorn the grave of a distinguished warrior with an ornamental covering of birchen bark. A small flag is also planted beside it and suffered to remain there until destroyed by the Spirit of the storm.

SONG OF THE TRAIL.

Come, brothers, come!
    Merry men are we,
Dashing through the forest shade,
    Weary though we be.
Hark! the bugle sounds, advance,
    Deeply rolls the battle-drum,
Draw the sword and poise the lance!
    Come, brothers, come!

Speed, brothers, speed!
    Follow where he flies,
Wheresoe'er his footsteps lead,
    There the pathway lies.
Hark! his shout is on the wind,
    Dash the rowels in your steed!
Brake and briar leave behind!
    Speed, brothers, speed!

Slow, brothers, slow;
    What is it ye crave?
"A comrade lies along the path,
    A corse without a grave."
Halt the column! friends, alight!
    Dig his bed the turf below!

We will trace the trail to-night;
   Slow, brothers, slow.

On, brothers, on!
   Draw the swords of men,
By his prey the wolf is known,
   Trace him to his den.
Follow bloom or follow blight,
   Battle lost or battle won,
Darkly blood must flow to-night, —
   On, brothers, on!

Strike, brothers, strike!
   Raise the battle-shout!
Tawny faces haunt the path,
   Savage eyes gleam out:
On upon them for your lives!
   Wrestle, pike with pike!
For your homes and for your wives
   Strike, brothers, strike!

CAMP AT TUSKEGEE, *Creek Nation, Ga.*

SONG OF THE INDIAN GIRL.

"The sun has left his place on high,
    The moon is in the glen,
And I must go toward yonder sky
    To keep the 'Panther's' den."

Thus sang beneath a rocking pine
    A maid of tawny hue,
And as she wove each measured line,
    She strung a bead of blue.

"Yes, I must go to yonder West,
    Where mountain daisies grow,
And arm the shaft and point its crest,
    And bear the loosened bow.

"And I must be a hunter's bride,
    And guide his swift canoe,
He swore it when at eventide
    He kissed my beads of blue.

"He swore it by the Spirit great
    That rides the troubled cloud,
And by his love and by his hate,
    And by his bearing proud."

Thus sang beneath a rocking pine
    A maid of tawny hue!
And as she wove each measured line
    She crushed a bead of blue.

"The moon has left her place on high,
    The *wolf* is in the glen,
I will not go to yonder sky,
    To keep the ' Panther's ' den.

"Upon the stream my bark shall swim,
    Beside the lone cuckoo,
And on the winds, as false as him,
    I'll cast my beads of blue."

SONG OF THE EMIGRANT INDIAN.

["And a treaty was entered into between the Commissioners and the tribe of the Sacs and Foxes, wherein the latter obligated themselves to retire beyond the Mississippi and never again to return."]

We pass beyond the river,
    A scorned and blighted thing,
We have dropped the bolt and quiver,
    And the bow knows not the string.

The voice whose tones were strongest
    Is hushed amid the strife,
The arm that fought the longest
    No more shall wield the knife.

Where met the best and proudest,
    Gather the faces pale,
Where rang the war-song loudest,
    Springeth a voice of wail.

The deer may leave his cover,
    And the white man sit alone,
For the hunter's toil is over,
    And the warrior's strength is gone.

We pass, O braves and daughters,
  We pass beyond the stream,
While a cloud comes o'er the waters,
  To shade the red man's dream.

We leave our homes behind us,
  The Spirit gave our race,
Nor friend nor foe may find us,
  For where will be our trace?

The wolf may range our mountains,
  The musk may scent the air,
And the beaver seek our fountains,
  There is none to set the snare.

No more the watch-dog nightly
  Will whine for our return,
And the wigwam's torch-light, brightly.
  No more for us shall burn.

We pass away in sorrow,
  As sets the sun's last beam,
But for us there comes no morrow,
  As we sink behind the stream.

INDIAN DIRGE.

[THE Northwestern Army, after following for many days the defeated and flying tribe of the Sacs and Foxes, at length encamped on the bank of the Mississippi. In the distance the last small remnant of their once-formidable foe were discovered chanting the death-dirge around a pole erected for the occasion.]

NEED-JE,* remnant of the last,
Gather round the cedar mast!
Tell the white man on the heath
Need-je sings the song of death!
Beat the tambor, shake the bells,
Scare him with the Prophet's spells!
Tell him — let the red man be —
Ptshe-mo-ko-mon, Puc-kee-ptshe. †

Sing! the *Hawk* hath left the skies,‡
Never more to stoop nor rise;
Broken is his mighty wing.
Sing the death-dirge — Need-je, sing!
Hovering o'er his prairie nest,
Bristles now the Eagle's crest;
Who is left to fight or flee?
Ptshe-mo-ko-mon, Puc-kee-ptshe.

* Indian.
† White man, go away.
‡ Black Hawk, an Indian chief, a prisoner in the hands of the whites.

Long Knife, Long Knife, tribe of fear,
Wipe the yager's crooked spear ; *
Let your vengeance now suffice,
Hush the gun that thunders twice : †
Raise no more the whoop of strife,
Bury deep the painted knife ! ‡
Foxes' last papoose are we, —
Ptshe-mo-ko-mon, Puc-kee-ptshe.

Pale-face, go, but not in rage.
Feed the Hawk within his cage !
If ye bind him wrist to wrist
Let the cord be silver twist,
Bondage such as once he knew
When ye gave him beads of blue :
Gird him not to burning tree,
Ptshee-mo-ko-mon, Puc-kee-ptshe.

* Bayonet. † Mortar. ‡ The sword.

NIGHT ON THE SANTA FÉ, FLORIDA.

'T is night within the leafy wood,
'T is night upon the restless flood,
And not a cloud is in the skies
Whose burning stars, like lover's eyes,
Watch brightly o'er the favored tree *
Which shades the rushing Santa Fé.
The wind that wooes the sunset hour
Is cradled on the sleeping flower,
Where twilight seemeth still to cling
Like fondness to a cherished thing.
It is the hour for misty dream
To rise along the haunted stream,
For minstrel hand with measured touch
To strike the lyre it loves so much,
While, like a bird of wandering wing,
Fond fancy hovers o'er the string.
And here, 't is here, like stag at bay,
The brave disputes the tangled way,
At midnight o'er the startled flood,
Yelling the vengeance call of blood.
In yonder hummock long and low
He darkly lurks — a restless foe,
Well pleased to cross the club of strife
With him who holds the "burnished knife." †

* Magnolia.   † The sword.

Oh, who would think, that linger here
Along these waters flashing clear,
That every ripple bright and blue
Has stained these shells with murder's hue?
This aged tree with moss o'ergrown
Hath seen the blow and heard the moan,
That hoary rock what tales could tell
Of them who fought and them who fell!

I heard a shout upon the wind,
Like cry of wolf that trails the hind,
I heard a shriek upon the lea,
Like terror's voice from wreck at sea,
While pale and horror-struck one came
To gasp "the deed without a name."
It was the hour when evening fair
Came down to close the eyes of care,
A father watched the sunset mild,
A mother rocked her sleeping child.
There as they sat, those happy few,
They heard the whoop — too well they knew.
The rifle blazed, the hatchet fell,
And did the deed I dare not tell.
I saw them by the moonlight ray,
As side by side in death they lay.
Upon the mother's pulseless breast
Chill slept the babe in dreamless rest,
While o'er the pillow where it laid
Slow oozed a stream the knife had made.

It slept, but oh! in death so fair,
I almost thought that life was there;
So fresh its lip of silent strain,
I almost dreamed 't would smile again.*

Bright forms who bask where Freedom's star
Burns in the Northern sky afar,
Whose darkest care is but to stay
Some wanton curl that dares to stray,
Whose deepest grief to weep at slight
From lover's hand on festive night!
When at the hearth of kindred ground
Ye pass the vesper kiss around,
And from the social evening fire
To dream of those ye love, retire,
Ere with the cheek of quiet rest
Ye make the conscious pillow blest,
Ere yields that form to slumber deep,
Sleep folding, — one might envy sleep, —
Could ye but let your fancy roam
One moment to our canvas home,
Where weary by the restless flood
The sentry walks the shore of blood;
Then ye might learn what toil hath he
Who guards the roaring Santa Fé.

* This is no fiction. During the summer of 1838, a party of savages entered a dwelling on the banks of the Santa Fé, Florida, and after murdering the elder portion of the occupants, took from the cradle an infant whose brains they dashed out, and left the babe, in a posture of repose, on the bosom of its dead mother.

SONG OF THE "CRIMSON HAND."

[AFTER a party of Florida Indians had been placed on board a transport destined to carry them from their homes, the boat by some accident grounded immediately opposite the Fort at Tampa Bay, Florida. During the night they were held in this durance, these savages consoled themselves by chanting a sort of chorus which alternated with a variety of sounds, some of which were extremely wild, and others of an order deeply melancholy.]

THE voice of blood went forth,
  Up from the border line,
It thrilled the sea from South to North,
  And it shook the forest pine.

"Rouse up, ye warrior band,
  And join the song of blood,
The song ye hear of the 'Crimson Hand,'
  We pour along the flood!
The Spirit whom we love
  Mutters in thunder low;
Hark! to the words he speaks above, —
  Woe to the pale-face! woe!"

Stern voices wildly sang
  In rude but measured strain;
Like armor's clang, the descant rang
  Athwart the troubled main.

"The knife is stained with red,
　　The battle-axe is ground,
And moulded is the poisoned lead
　　That rankles in the wound.
No more we chase the hare,
　　We hunt no more the roe,
A nobler toil henceforth we share, —
　　Woe to the pale-face! woe!"

　　'T was a deep and mournful strain!
　　　　Slow as the measured tread,
　　When moves the train on the tented plain,
　　　　To the roll of music dead.

"His brother sitteth not
　　Beside the council-fire,
The hummock heard the deathly shot
　　That parted son and sire.*
Unto our palm-leaf home
　　They came to seek the foe,
They came — they fell — who bid them come?
　　Woe to the pale-face! woe!"

　　'T was a chant of strange turmoil!
　　　　The planter caught the sound,

---

* At the battle of the Okeechubbee, which took place in Florida on the 25th of December, 1837, it is stated that the son of Colonel Gentry, of the Missouri Volunteers, was wounded by the same ball which proved fatal to the life of his father.

And the man of toil forsook his soil,
    And fled for the guarded ground.

" 'T is ours to lie in wait,
    For the reaper's team at morn;
We burst the cribs of them we hate,
    And we crush the standing corn.
Amid the ripening grain
    We dance with merry toe,
Chanting beside the tiller slain,
    Woe to the pale-face! woe!"

    The panther fled the sound,
        Stood still the frighted deer,
    And on the bound the startled hound
        Turned back and crouched with fear.

" We watch the road beside,
    To spill the purple flood,
And when with hate our lips are dried,
    We lap the curdled blood.
We prowl the woods at night,
    We scalp the sleeping foe,
We live for vengeance and the white, —
    Woe to the pale-face! woe!"

    Like screech of wild curlew,
        It passed the bed of rest,
    And the mother knew and closer drew
        The infant to her breast.

"Around the couch we creep,
  Yelling the war-whoop wild,
We stab the mother in her sleep,
  And choke the shrieking child.
The fagot pile we raise,
  To burn their wigwam low,
Fierce shouting o'er the spreading blaze,
  Woe to the pale-face! woe!"

  The mount with voice of wail
    Prolonged the notes of dread,
  And in the vale the planet pale
    Went down and set in red.

"Ours are the hands to dare,
  Fast fettered though they be,
For free we were and free we are,
  And lo! we *will* be free!
Unconquered to the last,
  Out from our homes we go:
We hurl our curses on the blast, —
  Woe to the pale-face! woe!"

TAMPA BAY, *Florida*, 1837.

PALE EYE ON WING OF STARLIGHT RAYS.

[WRITTEN at Fort Russell, Florida, on the departure of a column of troops organized for the punishment of a party of Indians implicated in the murder of the wife of an officer, together with a portion of the escort accompanying a wagon-train from Fort Wheelock to Fort King. The circumstances which gave rise to this expedition involve an episode of the war, a relation of which will not prove uninteresting to the reader.

In the early part of the Florida War, Lieutenant Montgomery, a young officer of the United States Infantry, stationed at Newport, Kentucky, solicited and received the hand of the fair Miss Taylor, a young lady extensively known among the polite circles of that city, both for beauty of person and refinement of manners. On the departure of Lieutenant Montgomery for Florida, the young bride was persuaded to accompany him, and in due course of time arrived at Fort Wheelock, one of the interior posts at which her husband was stationed. To relieve the *ennui* of garrison life, she accepted an invitation from her friend, Mrs. Hopson of Fort King, to visit that post, and with a small escort accompanying a train with provisions, in charge of Lieutenants Sherwood and Hopson, started, one pleasant morning, on the anticipated excursion. The first intimation of any disaster accruing to the party was the arrival of the animal used by Mrs. Montgomery, which came galloping into the garrison without a rider, followed by several of the mounted men, who stated that the train had been attacked at a creek some three miles distant from Fort Wheelock, which report was corroborated, soon afterward, by the arrival of Lieutenant Hopson himself.

The long roll was immediately beat, and a party of mounted men detached to the spot.

On arriving at the scene of danger, it was ascertained that the enemy had fled. Near the wagons, the horses of which were slain, lay the breathless remains of Lieutenant Sherwood and such portion of the guard as had possessed sufficient courage to remain with him. The prostrate and bleeding form of Mrs. Montgomery was stretched near them. She was still breathing, but unconscious, and expired soon afterward. She had been divested by the Indians of her riding habit, but had suffered no peculiar acts of inhumanity at their hands. The frock-coat of Lieutenant Sherwood had also been abstracted from his person.

Soon after the occurrence, one of the teamsters, who managed to escape, stated several interesting particulars in regard to the transaction to which he professed to be an eye-witness. The Indians were concealed in a dense hummock fringing the borders of the creek, and on the approach of the train directed a well-aimed volley at the mounted men who preceded the wagons. Lieutenant Sherwood immediately dismounted, formed his men, and directed Mrs. Montgomery to alight and take refuge in one of the covered wagons for better security to her person. At the same time Lieutenant Hopson was ordered to return as speedily as possible to Fort Wheelock for reinforcements. Meanwhile Lieutenant Sherwood, together with the few men who remained with him, closed around the wagon containing the unfortunate young lady, in front of which they fell, one by one, beneath the murderous fire of the concealed enemy.

It was during this period, hoping to escape unseen amid the general *mêlée*, that the teamster who drove the wagon in which Mrs. Montgomery was located, all the horses of which had been shot down, withdrew the young lady through the rear of the vehicle, and with his arm around her fragile figure attempted their precarious flight. The effort was partially successful. They had succeeded in gaining a considerable distance on the path of retreat, when they were discovered by the enemy, who, suddenly issuing from the covert, pursued them with shouts and rapid strides. Fear might have added wings to the flying fugitives, had not the long riding-dress worn by the young lady interfered to obstruct her progress. Entangled within its trailing folds, she frequently fell, and the painful fact soon became evident to her companion that the time thus lost enabled the enemy to gain upon them, and should he continue to remain with his young charge, the fate *of* both was sealed. Again she fell; and as the war-whoop approached nearer, mingled with sounds of savage laughter, the terrified wagoner fled, leaving the unfortunate lady to her fate. Only once he glanced behind him, his eyes being attracted in that direction by a piercing shriek, when he perceived the forlorn girl, who had regained her feet, running directly toward the enemy. Bewildered with terror, she courted the danger which gave rise to it, and no doubt soon afterward received the death-wounds which prostrated her on the spot where she was subsequently discovered. On receiving news of this disaster at Fort Russell, a post contiguous to Fort Wheelock, an expedition, consisting of an hundred men of the Second United States Infantry, was fitted out, and proceeded to scour the country bordering the Oklawaha, where the marauding band was supposed to dwell. Under the compelled guidance of three squaws, who were surprised and captured while gathering *counti* roots in a neighboring wood, the troops succeeded in discovering a camp of one of the principal chiefs named *Alec Tustenuggee*. The Indians, however, had abandoned their huts, which were found to contain not only an ample supply of provisions, but also articles of plunder taken by them in their predatory excursions, among which were recognized the frock-coat of Lieutenant Sherwood, and a remnant of broadcloth, identified as a portion of the riding-habit which had belonged to the victim bride whose sad fate was so deeply deplored.

The troops proceeded to burn the encampment, and after an unsuccessful and harassing pursuit of the offending party, at the expiration of some ten days, returned to Fort Russell.

Although the main object of the expedition was unattained, yet it was not wholly without satisfactory results, as it culminated in the destruction of the Indian village, and the capture of three of the females belonging to it, one of whom proved to be the favorite wife of Alec Tustenuggee, the renegade chief.]

PALE Eve on wing of starlight rays
   Flits o'er the hostile glen;
Too broadly glares our watch-fire's blaze, —
   Rouse up, my weary men!

Yon flame, like Love, though seeming bright,
    Betrays us with its charms;
The *archer* aims beneath its light, —
    To arms, my boys! to arms!

He comes as comes the summer's breath,
    As softly steals the doe;
Draw out the sabre from its sheath,
    And wait the wary foe!
Think not your couch, like woman's bed,
    Is rife with soft alarms;
The yell of blood ye hear instead;
    To arms, my boys! to arms!

Rouse up, and let no coward fear
    Arraign your bearing high!
Fond Pity sheds her choicest tear
    To see a soldier die,
And when the life-flame burneth dim
    Within the breast it warms,
'T is Glory twines a wreath for him;
    To arms, my boys! to arms!

INDIAN MELODY.

Hark! his shout is on the air!
   Sound ye well may heed;
Woodman, to your home repair,
   Speed, hunter, speed!
" Daughter, why thy cheek so pale?"
   " Mother, whisper low;
I see him coming down the vale,
   The horrid shrieking foe!"
             Hark, &c.

Hunter, haste! and heed ye not
   Where the game hath fled;
Homeward to your lonely cot,
   Ere the knife be red!
" Now they launch upon the stream,
   Now they reach the shore,
Oh mother! how the hatchets gleam,
   And how the rifles roar!"
             Hark, &c.

Hunter, speed! call back the hound,
   Leave the stag at bay,
Ford the stream and gain the ground
   Where your children play!

"Mother, look! they come more nigh!"—
"How to save my child!—
I dare not stay, I dare not fly,
  They shriek so fierce and wild!"
                    Hark, &c.

THE FLIGHT.

[It was asserted, by some of the Florida prisoners, that a column of the pursuing army bivouacked one night on a spot immediately contiguous to the hiding-place of their retreating families, who escaped during the darkness from such dangerous proximity.]

"Brother!" — o'er a warrior's side
  Softly sung a forest bride : —
"Brother! spread the blanket warm, —
  We are houseless mid the storm!
  But the pale-face — name of fear —
  Thanks! may never venture here;
  'T is the hummock green and wild,
  Only known to Nature's child!"

"Sister, hark! — 't is he — he comes!
  Listen to the signal drums!
  Know ye not his token sound?
  Death and danger hover round.
  Note his watch-fires through the pines, —
  We must leave our home of vines;
  Faint and weary though we be,
  Once again must rise and flee!"

"Brother! 'neath the spreading palm,
  We have scattered leaves of balm,

And our children, worn with care,
Softly now are sleeping there.
Wet and rugged was the way
Over which they passed to-day ;
We have wandered many a mile,
Let, oh let us rest awhile."

" Sister! sterner couch is ours,
Than the bed of scented flowers ;
We are cast on Fortune's flood ;
They are near who seek our blood.
Rouse the infant from its dream ;
Leap the bank and cross the stream ;
Though the night is on the plain,
We must tread the trail again."

THE FALL OF MONIAC.

[AMONG the many brave spirits whose remains lie buried in the sanguinary glades of Florida, few have fallen more lamented than the heroic Moniac. He was by birth a Creek, and by profession a soldier; uniting the valor of his tribe with the scientific skill attained by an education at the United States Military Academy, his success in the field in almost every instance was triumphant. Although the breaking out of the Creek War seemed calculated to estrange his affections from his whilom adopted brethren, yet his friendship for the whites remained constant to the last. Soon after the termination of the Creek campaign in the summer of 1836, Moniac, together with other warriors of his nation, accompanied Colonel Lane in his ill-fated expedition against the refractory Seminoles, and such was the trust reposed in the intrepidity of this daring chief, that he bore rank with the officers of the army of the United States. From this expedition Moniac never returned. He fell in an impetuous charge at the head of his feathered warriors, in the autumn of 1836.]

THERE rang a voice o'er the warrior's clay
   Outstretched on the field of death,
And I caught the chant which it seemed to say,
   Mid the pause of the battle's breath: —

"Warrior! why sleep'st thou here?
   Unclose thy deep-sealed eye!
The battle-shout is on the ear,
   And the death-shaft hurtles by.

"Unsheathe thy flashing brand!
　　Let the lightning scan its sire!
Spread forth in might thy tawny hand, —
　　Let the valiant one retire.

"The tocsin thunders deep,
　　And the charger paws the plain!
Up! rouse thee from thy listless sleep,
　　That the war-tide swell again!

"'T is for the twig to bow,
　　When the storm-cloud sweeps the skies,
But a prouder, loftier thing wert thou!
　　Warrior, awake! arise!"

Then a gentler voice, with a softer tone,
　　Swelled where the warrior lay;
And I caught the words as wild and lone,
　　They chimed o'er the pulseless clay: —

"Sleep, brother; from thy cheek
　　Life's shadowy cloud hath past!
No longer there the storm shall wreak
Its wrath — nor thou, a mortal weak,
　　Cope with the pelting blast.

"Than thine what choicer bed
　　For a soldier's weary frame?
With the flowery earth beneath thy head,

The bright blue heaven above thee spread,
  And around thee hearts of flame.

"Rest! for the race is run,
  Rest! for the strife is o'er;
With crimson beams to-morrow's sun
May light the war-clouds looming dun —
  But thou shalt toil no more.

"Thine is the lot to die
  And share a household grave;
To slumber where thy fathers lie,
Where rang of yore their battle-cry,
  By Withlacoochee's wave.

"Far happier than thy band,
  Fast scattering to the wind,
Urged helpless to some foreign strand,
An alien from their own fair land,
  Thou shalt remain behind.

"Where moss and wild-flowers creep
  Along thy native hills,
Regardless of the tocsin deep,
As sleep the brave, so thou shalt sleep,
  Mid the music of the rills."

THE MISTAKEN VOLUNTEER.

> "On gorgeously they come,
> With plumes low stooping on their winding way,
> And banners glancing in the sun's bright ray."
> *Song of the Field.*

> "A change came o'er the spirit of my dream." — BYRON.

Oh! once I was a soldier,
   And very trim was I;
I loved to hear the rattling drum
   And watch the colors fly.
It was my pride and glory
   To march along the town,
And watch from every window
   Some pretty eye look down.

My uniform was scarlet,
   My plume was snowy white,
And golden mounted was my sword,
   Whose blade was very bright.
My steed, he was a war-horse
   It was my pride to sit,
For he wore a broidered saddle,
   And he champed a gilded bit.

Oh! life of martial honor,
   Mingled with love's array!

One shining button on my breast
   Wrought more than words could say.
I sat beside the maiden,
   And I never spoke the while,
But I let the Eagle glisten,
   And I saw the damsel smile.

Thrice blest! Thou gentle fortune
   Which crowned those halcyon hours,
When hand in hand with sighing love
   Mars sat in Beauty's bowers!
When the mirror of the soldier
   Was set in woman's face,
And he was most the hero
   Who wore the finest lace.

But ah! a change has happened —
   Sad, sad reverse for me!
I went unto the distant war,
   Over the distant sea.*
Say, have I not, sweet ladies,
   Just reason to demur,
For I draw a rusty sabre,
   And I wear a rusty spur.

---

* From the description which he gives of himself, it is presumed this unfortunate son of Mars must have *volunteered*, at some time or other, for an " excursion ", from the land of milk and honey to the fastnesses of recent Indian notoriety, situated among the interminable swamps of hostile Florida.

Where are my dreams of glory?
  Dissolved in marsh and mire;
Where is the glittering torch of fame?
  Gone out like an Indian's fire.
The trappings of my courser?
  Stol'n by the thieving foe;
And I ride without a saddle,
  And I march without a shoe.

Oh maids of former hours,
  Who blest me with your sighs,
I've not a single button left
  To glad your gentle eyes!
My plume is in a cane-brake,
  A thorn-bush wears my vest,
And my coat hath lost its tinsel, —
  What care ye for the rest?

Alas! in search of glory
  How foolish thus to roam!
I'll take my pack upon my back
  And steer again for home;
Though doomed at every window
  Some well-known voice to hear,
"Do but behold him, sister, —
  Yon ragged volunteer!"

CAMP AT SUWANEE SPRINGS, *Florida*, 1838.

SONG OF THE OKEE-FEE-NOKEE.

[WRITTEN in answer to a playful banter that the author could not produce a rhyme to "Okee-fee-nokee." In order to a correct understanding of the subjoined lines, it may not be deemed inappropriate to insert a note explanatory of them.

The Okee-fee-nokee swamp, some one hundred and twenty miles in circuit, situated on the southern boundary of Georgia, was a region almost wholly unknown until a late period of the Florida War, when it was occasionally visited by parties of troops, in pursuit of the refractory Seminoles who were concealed in its almost inaccessible fastnesses. Its borders fringed with high walls of cypress, interspersed with dense shrubbery, served as a barrier to exclude its inner recesses from the outside world. These hidden fastnesses could only be reached through the agency of native guides, over narrow and carefully concealed paths, termed trails.

It was in the month of December, 1838, that Captain T. Morris, of the Second Infantry, by direction of General Floyd, commanding the Okee-fee-nokee district, accompanied by a detachment of troops with a guide, attempted to explore this inhospitable region. Entering at a point where the trail presented signs sufficiently distinct to follow, the troops for several miles were enabled to plod their way through the mazes of the outer belt without encountering any serious obstacle to oppose their progress. The path, however, gradually became less distinct, until, at length, it was totally obliterated. Surrounded by impervious thickets they were obliged to have recourse to their hatchets in order to extricate themselves. On emerging, over this improvised path, from the surrounding underwood, they gained a slight acclivity from which the interior of the swamp presented a panoramic view sufficiently picturesque to reward the adventurers for the labor attending its invasion.

Stretches of low land covered with cypress, undulating knolls of pine whose scraggy trunks were encircled by the morning-glory, the passion-flower, the jessamine, and the climbing clematis, isolated masses of the tasseled cane, and impervious thickets studded with the gnarled oak and fan-leaved palmetto, contrasted with the gleam of open waters, dotted with small islands, and broad fields of waving grass which concealed, beneath a veil of verdure, the unruffled but treacherous element which slept beneath them.

After pausing for a while to notice the varied elements of this wild scenery, the troops were again put in motion, and, guided by the compass, pursued, as near as intervening obstacles would permit, the intended route ; sometimes cutting their way through crowding canes and the prickly cactus, sometimes creeping upon their hands and knees over a narrow path — the trail of a bear or an alligator — flanked on either side by thick underbrush surmounted by low tangled vines so closely interlaced that the possibilty of assuming an upright position was precluded for hours, and again wading waist-deep, through the grass of an overflowed prairie.

Progress along that portion of the swamp occupied by cypress-trees, it was not difficult to maintain, so long as due care was manifested to plant the foot upon one of the exposed roots or knees which rose in close contiguity to each other, but, should a false step be made, the unfortunate individual would sink in the yielding surface from which it was difficult to extricate himself. Like care had to be manifested in traversing the submerged prairies or meadows, as the footing was insecure, the water frequently deepened as he advanced, and he had either to return, or shape his course toward one of the small islands, for a temporary resting-place.

It was on the third day of the march that the troops suddenly encountered one of these prairies, which stretched like a vast amphitheatre before them. As it was several miles in circuit, the attempt was made to pass directly over it, but with indifferent success. The water had gradually deepened, and when the troops were nearly half way over, it was found utterly impracticable to proceed further in the required direction. It had been raining violently throughout the day, and the men, wet and weary, were not in a condition to retrace their steps.

In this dilemma, fortunately for the command, a small island was discerned at a short distance from the left of the line. A solitary cypress, from the branches of which drooped long gray ringlets of moss, alone marked its locality, so little was the spot elevated above the surface of the submerged prairie. Altering their course, the troops soon reached the desired haven. The island was oval in shape, of small dimensions, and carpeted with short dense greensward, but, with the exception of that lone denizen of the swamp before mentioned, not a tree nor a shrub grew upon it.

Weary and weak and cold, without the means of procuring fuel, but thankful for a spot to rest upon, the men took possession of the premises and covering themselves with garments of moss purloined from the wardrobe of the friendly cypress, bivouacked there for the night. Early the next morning, just previous to the evacuation of the island, the troops simultaneously inaugurated an impromptu dance, for the purpose of exciting circulation in their benumbed limbs, which the coldness of the night previous had reduced to a state of semi-paralysis. During the performance of this " prompt manœuvre" (not laid down in Army Tactics) the entire structure was observed to partake of an oscillatory motion, giving rise to the belief that its foundations were neither of rock or sand.

This supposition was afterward corroborated by an experiment suggested by Dr. Williams, the Assistant Surgeon of the detachment. A pole, prepared for the purpose by cutting a limb from the cypress-tree and divesting it of its redundant branches, was forced through the leafy surface to the depth of some three feet, after which no further obstruction impeded its insertion to its entire length.

Judgment thereupon was pronounced that the so-called island was nothing more nor less than a *floating* mass of decayed vegetable matter; and from its tendency to shake or quiver, it received the appellation of " Trembling Island." Such are the circumstances which gave rise to the name mentioned in the text, and which, also, may tend to explain the allusion made to those other spots or islands " as yet undiscovered by *Morris* or *Floyd.*"

It is not the purpose of this note to exhibit further, in detail, the varied phases encountered by the troops during their sojourn in this inhospitable region. It is deemed sufficient to remark, that after leaving the island, with some difficulty not unattended with peril, they were enabled to secure sure footing on an adjacent shore, where, after a seven days' ordeal, passed in the pleasant pastime of creeping, leaping, and floundering, they at length gained *terra firma* on the outside border of the swamp, much to the gratification of the parties concerned.]

You dare me to sing of the Okee-fee-nokee —
  The word to be sure is uncouth to the ear,
And yet you may still (if the rhymes do not choke
    ye,)
  Make ready to read or be silent to hear.
    You say 't is the swamp, sir,
    So dismal and damp, sir,
Whose intricate windings you wish me to show,
    With its lake of the red man,
    And shore of the dead man
Who perished by famine or fell by the blow.

Do you see yonder cypress? 'T is on "Trembling
    Island,"
  Which name from its character aptly it gets,
Because should you step there, supposing it dry land,
  'T is twenty to one but your isle oversets.
    Like a ship without breezes,
    It rocks as it pleases,
Sad footing for marching men, likely to drown,
    And often they say, sir,
    Would have floated away, sir,
Were it not for that *cypress*, which anchors it down.

You 've read of the stream which they name from
    St. Mary?
  That hummock of saplings its head-waters know,
And you 've heard of the birds of the famed "Mother
    Carey!"
    They feed in yon cane till to "chickens" they
        grow;

And the gentle *Nautilus*,
(This measure will kill us,)
Freights yonder his bark e'er to ocean he sails,
    While the rough alligator,
    The wonder of " natur,"
Bends hither his course when he changes his scales.

Look now at the west where the day-star is streaming,
    Like the light of an eye o'er a scene it enjoyed,
Oh, yonder are spots, in the far distance gleaming,
    As yet undiscovered by Morris or Floyd.
    By the light of the sunset,
    There ready for fun set
The nut-cracking squirrel and moss-eating hare,
    And blithe 'neath the moon-ray
    The fox and the coon play,
While the wolf dances round with the cub of the bear.

And there, at the mention the bull-frog stops leaping,
    The snake seeks its hole, and the hornet its hive,—
Dwells the red-handed Ghost who hath kept and is
        keeping
    The corse of the Florida War still alive;
    And who laughs every night, sir,
    To see the sad plight, sir,
Of the leg-weary soldier — a mud-stricken thing —
    Like Araby's Daughter, bogged,
    Helpless, and water-logged,
Oh, 't is of the Okee-fee-nokee I sing!

HUMMOCK, OKEE-FEE-NOKEE, *February* 21, 1839.

PROMISCUOUS POEMS.

THE POWERS OF WOMAN.

[FRAGMENT from "Ben and Elbert," an early poem, written at West Point Academy, an episode from which, "The Dreaming Boy," is inserted among "The Songs of the Bower."]

A DREAM of woman! I have seen the hour
   When I have bowed before her idol shrine,
And worshiped, pagan-like, as to a power
   Derived from Godhead, sinless, pure, divine;
Whether in courtly hall or secret bower
   Mid the deep grove where flaunting myrtles twine,
Where'er her altar stood, 't was all the same,
So it was blessed by woman's sainted name.

I 've stood a gazer in the joyous crowd,
   With beauty gathered round, and light, and song,
Where the wild burst of laughter echoed loud,
   And eyes shone out, as if to light along
The reveler's mazy pathway — and I 've bowed
   My knee like an adorer in that throng,
And in the drunkenness of passion given
Madly to woman attributes of Heaven.

I learned Love's language — like an artist wrought
   Upon my nature till 't was moulded well,

Attuned my voice melodiously, and sought
  O'er ponderous tomes for words of dulcet swell
To lisp in meet accordance — when I'd fraught
  My tongue with studied phrases, soft to tell,
In deep recess, with none but her to hear,
It was my wont to breathe them in her ear.
      .

Oh, there was one whom I remember well!
  One when my sorrows like my years were few,
With whom, so strong her fascination's spell,
  The fleeting hours like passing moments flew;
Fanned by her breath, with her in secret dell,
  My island harp its inspiration drew,
And ever thus, charmed by the siren's lure,
"Oh maiden bright," I sang, "Oh maiden pure!"

And did I love her? let me press my heart
  And gain the answer from that prompter rare!
Ah no! it yields no quick impetuous start,
  No thrill disturbs the equal pulses there;
When souls *adore*, love acts a *silent* part;
  I breathed her name as I would breathe a prayer.
Soft murmuring, when she lit my vision's sky,
"Oh, cloud-bright dream! Oh, rainbow deity!"
  . . . .

And all was mockery — vilest of mockeries —
  A wild, wild vision, maddening as it mocks!
Is it not thus? answer, thou thing of sighs,
  Wiles, cunning, treachery, Nature's paradox!
Dost thou not make of man a sacrifice,
  Wind him, — aye, even as thou dost thy locks,

To suit thy fickle purpose, — curdle, rile
His very heart's blood with thy haunting smile?

Have I not listened to thy oft-pledged word
   And proved thee, as thou art, a thing of air?
Gathered thee to my bosom as a bird
   Garners her brood, and found a serpent there?
Have I not felt the throes of hope deferred,
   Pangs, writhing pangs to which 't were bliss — despair —
Which, should I will to picture, words would fail?
All this? and yet I *love* thee — woman, hail!

'T is ever thus, has been, will be with man!
   Ambition, wealth, doomed for a smile to barter;
The proudest he who best can flirt a fan,
   The noblest knight the " the order of the garter;"
Leader alike of hosts and woman's van,
   In war a hero, and in love a martyr.
What has steeled heart 'gainst heart — whole kingdoms stirred?
A breath? nay, lighter far — a woman's word.

What was the weapon conquered Cæsar's foe?
   What but the fire from Cleopatra's eye;
What laid the halls of haughty Priam low,
   The thunderbolt of Jove — or Helen's sigh?
When was the hour the world was doomed to woe
   And the world's lord to death? Let Eve reply!
Woman! man's keenest scourge, man's kindest nurse,
Thou art his blessing — and thou art his curse!

THE CALIFORNIA TRANSPORT.

[WRITTEN, soon after the discovery of gold in California, on the departure of a transport from New York, containing troops and other passengers, destined for San Francisco, *via* Cape Horn.]

THY rising streamers kiss the coaxing breeze,
   The day is breaking where the clouds hung dark,
For many a moon thy home is on the seas, —
         Fill, — and away, thou bark!

Within thy thick-ribbed sides are stores of weight;
   The gay-robed soldier and the trader plain
Together crowd thy deck, — a motley freight
         Of gallantry and gain.

Some have embarked full buoyant with the dream
   Of wealth amassed by toil of diver bold, —
Rich jewels glistening far 'neath crystal stream
         Hallowed by legends old.

Tempted are some by tale of shining ore
   Hid in the wombs of far Francisco's land,
Or brighter spots on Sacramento's shore
         Sprinkled with golden sand.

Some have set out whose roving bosoms burn
   To feel the freshness of a foreign sky, —

Of these, of all, some shall at length return, —
        Some have gone forth to die.

And they are with thee, — thou shalt rock their head
  Whose smile is placid and whose voice is mild;
Deal gently with them on their heaving bed,
        Thou bark of ocean wild!

Thy wings shall waft thee swiftly o'er the stream
  Whose constant current moves by mystic sway;*
Bright isles shall greet thee with their dangerous gleam
        Upon thy flashing way.

High on the coast where swift Magellan's tide
  Unites two oceans — mightiest of the sphere —
Strange tawny bands shall pause to see thee glide
        Along thy proud career.

Thy frame shall quiver where the mountain surge
  Replies in thunder to the monsoon's roar,
And the wild sea-fowl screams the sailor's dirge
        By Patagonia's shore.

And thou shall sleep becalmed, till heart shall tire,
  Where the earth's axle shows its least incline,
While glows the tropic sun with equal fire
        Along the burning line.

    * Gulf Stream.

Yes! waves shall lift thee and wild winds shall
  sweep;
And Ocean's monsters flash across thy way;
Yet thou shalt cope undaunted with the deep,—
    A wrestler stern at play.

Then onward! over the majestic seas!
 The day is breaking where the clouds hung dark,
Columbia's banner flutters on the breeze,—
    Fill,— and away, thou bark!

THE BRIDE'S LAST SLEEP.

She died as dies the beam of day
   Along a gem of cost;
Life's glorious ray — all quenched it lay —
   Alas! the loved and lost!

She died as dies the passion-flower
   Transferred to climes of strife;
Nurtured in warm and genial bower,
   Who could expect its life?

She died as dies some plaintive turn
   In dreams of music's strain;
The ear may list, — the heart may yearn, —
   It ne'er comes back again.

She died as dies Eve's roseate light
   Far o'er the billows dim;
One look — and melting into night
   Her smile went down on *him*.

She died? no, no, though mortal eye
   Might seem such change to see,
She could not die! in yonder sky
   She lives — and lives for *thee*.

CHANGE.

Change, 't is penciled in hues of light
   On all which the eye can view!
'T is stamped on the silver brow of night,
   On the crest of the morning blue,
On the golden cloud in the sunset west,
   On the bow which spans the lea;
There's a change for the worst or a change for
      the best
   For each and all but me.

A voice of change for the hunter's ear!
   'T is heard in the hound's deep bay;
The warrior too that tone may hear,
   It rings in the trumpet's bray.
A voice of change on the autumn air
   To the bird of pinion free,
To the forest, the brook, the glen,— but where
   Is a voice of change for me?

A sound of change for the placid deep!
   It swells on the tempest's roar;
For the sailor's bride in her lonely sleep,
   It chants from the wreck-strewn shore.

The breathing lute and the sounding hall,
  The blossom which scents the tree,
There 's a change for each and a change for all, —
  But where is a change for me?

Give me the meed of the bosom's dread,
  To cope with the flashing spear!
To weep unsoothed by the voiceless dead!
  To watch by the midnight bier!
Give me the laugh of reckless mirth,
  Though hollow and wild it be!
A dirge to moan o'er a desolate hearth,
  So thou bring *change* to me!

THE CONDEMNED CHRISTIAN.

THE ARENA.

[A PORTAL of the arena opened and the combatant, with a mantle thrown over his face and figure, was led in surrounded by soldiery. The lion ramped and roared against the bars of its den. At this sight the guard put a sword and buckler into the hands of the Christian, and he was left alone. — SALATHIEL.]

I.

WILD swelled the shout, and high
　　Flourished the trumpet's tone;
The arches answered the vassal cry,
Plume and purple came floating by,
　　And the King was on his throne.

II.

Around the regal chair
　　There were brows with garlands dressed,
Some, never dimmed by a thought of care,
Shadowed alone by their sun-bright hair,
　　Some that the helmet pressed.

III.

Again to the welkin wide
　　Sounded a blast of fear,

Slowly the columns wheeled aside,
And the victim was seen, with his bonds untied,
  Leaning upon his spear.

IV.

"Have ye gone? Have ye all out passed?"
  'T was a herald's warning tone;
One plume yet fluttered in the blast,
It stooped, it vanished, 't was the last, —
  And the Christian stood alone.

V.

Now gird thee for the fight,
  Thou of the fearless band!
Thine arm must cope with a foe of might,
No *human feet*, save thine, to-night
  May tread the arena's sand.

VI.

He raised his eyes on high,
  And breathed a hurried prayer,
The earthly monarch bade him die,
But he knew, as he scanned that holy sky,
  A mightier King was there.

VII.

Watch ye that captive slave,
  Prince of a royal line?
Give but thy sceptre's slightest wave,
And a thousand spears will flash to save!
  But the monarch made no sign.

VIII.

Then blushing cheeks grew pale,
  And mid that bright array
Love whispered an unheeded tale,
And the Roman maid withdrew her veil,
  Unconscious of display.

IX.

Aye! silence reigned around!
  And there burst a hollow roar,
And the arches echoed the thrilling sound,
As a lion loosed, with a sudden bound,
  Leaped from his grated door.

X.

Crouching with slow advance,
  He rears his bristling mane;
He hath measured his foe with a flaming glance,
He springs! — and the captive's shining lance
  Weareth a crimson stain!

XI.

"Huzza!" so swelled the song,
  "For the lord of the lance and lair!"
And the arches shook with the plaudits strong,
And the King passed out from the cheering throng,
  For he feared the God of prayer.

THE OCEAN.

How fair the main as, bathed in crimson dye,
    The weary billow seeks the sunset isle,
Its rage forgetting 'neath that placid sky,
    As if 't were bound beneath a siren's wile!
Like man's dark mind full oft where tempests lie,
    Till soothed to peace by woman's twilight smile.
Where is thy child, the Storm-king, placid deep?
Amid thy coral caverns doth he sleep?

My gaze is on thee! earnestly I stand,
    Watching thy waves' alternate ebb and flow;
Gently I feel my burning forehead fanned
    With breezes light which o'er thy surface blow;
How sweet the thoughts of home which, far from land,
    In yonder bark the wanderers must know!
That bark upon thy bosom seems to rest,
Calm as an infant on its mother's breast.

Of far, far bowers where climbs the clasping vine,
    And many a perfume breathes — thou art the token;
Thou call'st to mind the land of mirth and wine,
    As if a voice from Eastern groves had spoken.

Climes I have left ne'er more to call them mine;
  The minstrel boy still loves his lute, though broken,
For the remembered strains which once it gave —
And thus thou art to me, — sleep on, bright wave!

There is a sound of waters on mine ear!
  The Spirit of the tempest claims the lea;
The loud, wild lashing of the surge I hear, —
  The mountain-crest of foamy waves I see.
Hush, hush, thy roaring, — is the mother's tear
  Shed for her sailor-boy, but naught to thee?
Nay more, the fair-haired bride is on the main, —
Cease, cease thy rising! Ocean, sleep again.

Aye! hush thy roaring! — and a prouder swell
  As if in mockery burst on the shore,
Another, and another, — ha! that yell!
  'T is swelling yet, — while with a deeper roar
The surging billow chimed an answering knell,
  As if the sea-dog at old Ocean's door,
Watching for victims in his coral hall,
Knew 't was the voice of man — that frenzied call!

Yea! 't was the wildering shriek of mortals where
  The elements together madly strove;
The proud of heart, the strong in arm were there,
  And lips but formed for breathing vows of love, —

All, all, from the rough tars who nobly dare,
　Unshrinking o'er the shattered deck to rove,
To the fair girl who lisped in accents mild, —
Oh! these are not thy victims, Ocean wild!

Onward and onward bounding, "like a thing
　Of life," that gallant bark still held its way.
As on still moves the eagle though his wing,
　Broken, no more upon the breeze may play.
While the frail maiden to the mast did cling,
　With her white cheek washed by the breaker's spray;
Onward and onward bounding dashed the bark!
The sea birds wheeled — the billows grew more dark.

A voice came o'er the waters, and it rung
　Wildly — O God! *how* wildly — on the air
White drapery streamed which whiter hands had flung,
　And tresses unconfined were floating there.
Upon a mountain surge the life-bark hung —
　A moment paused and then descended — where?
There's death mid thy receptacles, — the brave,
The beautiful are thine, — roll on, dark wave!

DESULTORY RHYMES.*

Ladies and gentlemen, all who assemble here,
    Pretty and witty and sprightly and gay,
Too kind to be cruel, too plain to dissemble here,
    Pause for a moment and list to my lay.
        What shall I say to you,
        So I can play to you,
        All in a way to you
        Pleasing to hear?
        My lute, ye may like it not,
        But if I strike it not
How may its music be judged by your ear?

Gathered ye are from all parts of the town to-night,
    In spite of the cloud which grew heavy with snow,
Skies may have tempests but may not a frown to-night
    Shade for one moment the light of a brow.
        Feasts intellectual,
        Without being sexual,
        Are surely effectual,
        To drive away care.

---

* Sent *incog.* to a Society in Providence, R. I., composed principally of young ladies, who were made, erroneously, to suppose the author was one of their own number.

Whatever they set me to,
None shall e'er get me to
Give up the pleasure this evening I share.

Faces there are which are fit for a painter here,
  Some with the furrow which sadness hath worn.
Some like the rose-leaf, and some of hues fainter
    here,
  And some like the lily, which shrinks from the
    morn.
    But, ladies, your faces,
    Whatever their graces,
    It sure not my place is
    To rhyme upon now;
    Lest you find it unpleasant,
    And it call from some present
  A tear to the cheek or a blush to the brow.

What amusement more chaste, which should one be
    inclined to,
Than list'ning to thoughts which are aptly conveyed
In prose or in verse if, like me, you 've a mind to
  Bow down and invoke the bewildering maid.
    This, ladies, oh this is,
    To Mothers and Misses,
    The sweetest of blisses
    Which letters e'er gave;
    But pleasure is fleeting,
    Remember, and cheating,
  As Time "slowly beats the dead march to the
    grave."

And now from your numbers I know that you
   single me,
 My name and my nature is bandied about,
But round your bright circle though much ye may
   gingle me,
 I smile at the thought that you'll ne'er find me
   out.
   Lips ye may whisper,
   And tongues ye may lisp her,
   But harder and crisper
   The task is to do;
   Like an over-done pie-crust,
   The more that you try must
Appear the objection to biting it through.

CAROLINE OF ENGLAND.

[It was said at the coronation of George the Fourth, that the royal Caroline applied for admission to Westminster Abbey while the ceremony was taking place, but was forbidden to enter.]

Deep be thy rest, fair daughter
   Of Brunswick's haughty line,
A star o'er Albion's water
   Hath set no more to shine!

Why gave thy lord to story
   The faults that Fame should screen,
Oh, bride of regal glory,
   Consort — yet not a queen?

They who had fawned and flattered
   In worship at thy shrine,
How soon like leaves were scattered,
   When fortune ceased to shine!

Betrothed and yet forsaken,
   Supreme and but a slave,
Heiress of claims unshaken,
   Yet a wanderer of the wave!

A gorgeous crowd was kneeling
  Beside a monarch's chair,
While the deep anthem pealing
  Rolled on the scented air.

He sat mid vaults resounding,
  With the crown upon his brow,
Princes and peers surrounding —
  But where, oh! where wert thou?

Not where the right-arm wielded
  The sceptre and the sword,
His arm, which should have shielded
  Her who had called him lord.

But sick at heart and slighted,
  Out from the glittering ring,
Alone, with grief benighted,
  She stood a banished thing.

Amid that pomp and splendor
  Of Britain's regal day,
Was there no voice to render
  Homage to one away?

Mid the bright forms which glistened
  Along the Minster hall,
Was there no ear that listened
  To catch its mistress' call?

Alas the hour! unfriended,
  By jealous tongues belied,
Not one poor hand extended
  To hail a monarch's bride.

Weary and weak and pitied,
  Even in her robes of state,
She came — and unadmitted
  Stood at the Minster gate.

Bride sovereign, though forsaken,
  Proud partner of a throne,
Heiress of claims unshaken,
  She turned and wept alone.

Where then was knighthood sleeping?
  Shame to the belt and spur!
That a thousands brands outleaping
  Flashed not for Fame and her.

How may it read in story
  That the blades of broidered sheen,
Which struck for England's glory,
  Struck not for England's queen?

Then should the tocsin sounding
  Have rung in the pillared hall,
While martial shouts, rebounding,
  Echoed from dome to wall.

Then should the red cross gleaming,
  Have soared mid bayonets brown,
From British banners streaming
  To right a British crown;

Telling what doom awaited
  The lip that dared defame,
With tale by lust created,
  A sovereign's regal name.

Deep be thy rest, fair daughter
  Of Brunswick's haughty line!
A star o'er Albion's water
  Hath set no more to shine.

1838.

THE HYMN OF DEATH.

I am a monarch! flower and tree
   And earth and living thing —
Each, all are mine! Bow down to me!
   I am your priest and king.

No mark is proof, avails no flight,
   Against my seasoned bow;
I aim at youth with its footstep light,
   And age with its locks of snow.

I seek mid forms of glittering pride
   For the tone of laughter loud,
And it is my wont to steal aside
   The loveliest of the crowd.

Unto the couch of soft repose
   With stealthy tread I stray,
And I pause beside the lip of rose,
   And kiss its smile away.

I weave athwart the warrior's bed
   The mantles of the slain,
And I dye the thread with hues of red,
   As the battle sweeps the plain.

I ride upon the tempest dark,
   When the storm is on the lea,
Watching the sailor's quivering bark,
   As it breasts the surging sea.

It is my warning voice ye hear,
   When the thunder mutters low;
I flash afar my levin-spear,
   And ye see the lightning's glow.

I am a monarch! flower and tree
   And earth and living thing —
Each, all are mine! Bow down to me!
   I am your priest and king.

Ye may bar the gates of the Temple's wall,
   Yet I stand in your aisles of prayer;
Ye may crown your chief in the crowded hall,
   Yet I reign as your sovereign there.

Give way! I pass through your ranks of mirth,
   Pause with the festal breath!
I am the lord of all the earth, —
   I am the conqueror — Death!

THE IMP OF THE PALACE.

WRITTEN SOON AFTER THE CORONATION OF VICTORIA.

["EDWARD COTTON, a boy about thirteen years of age, was on Friday brought before the magistrates of Queen's Square police-office, charged with being found concealed in the New Palace. He said he had been twelve months in the palace and had seen and heard the Queen speak at all hours, both to her Ministers and her attendants."] — OLD COUNTRYMAN.

SUNSET like Hope is fading fast,
   Both seem to shun my prison cell,
While 'gainst the lattice beats the blast,
   Seeming to sound my funeral knell;
All Nature frowns, but what care I?
For her I lived, for her can die.

I may not bide this lonely grief —
   There is such anguish on my brain,
That I have listened, for relief,
   To hear the clanking of the chain
Which bars the door that shuts from me
All that I ever wished to see.

My hand is small and I can slide
   The iron from my wrist at will,
And in some darkened nook might hide,
   Secure from all my keepers still;

Had I but strength (as these I shake)
The fetters of my heart to break.

They tell me I 'm a simple youth,
　　And some, they say, believe me mad;
I know not wherefore, save in truth
　　I 'm but a poor unfriended lad,
Whose crime it was, a spright unseen,
To haunt the chamber of my queen.

I oft had heard it whispered round
　　That she was like an angel fair;
But on the day I saw her crowned,
　　The regal cheek seemed pale with care;
And I did long, from pomp aside,
To view again the nation's bride.

And so I hid where in her bower
　　She sat remote beyond the throng;
But oh that glance! it left no power
　　For after choice of right or wrong, —
It was so sweet to watch unseen,
And breathe and *be* where she had been;

Where she had paused awhile to stand,
　　And muse along the scented way!
For this ye load with chains my hand,
　　And wrest me from the light of day.
But there 's a light of memory left,
Of which I may not be bereft.

I've seen the idol of the throne,
   As few have seen, in smiles and tears,
And when no other eye, my own
   Watched o'er a form my heart reveres.
Whate'er my doom, this thought of joy
Still cheers Victoria's vassal boy.

SONG OF THE SEA.

My home is on the heaving sea,
   Beyond the breakers' roar,
And I never hear of danger near,
   Save when I see the shore.
My life is like a flashing car,
   And like a merry stave,
For I whirl along the deep — huzza ! —
   And I dance upon the wave.

Amid the calm, without a care
   For aught that earth can bring,
Wide-rocking in the idle air,
   I sit aloft and sing.
And when the squall booms fierce and far,
   Regardless of the gale,
I climb the slippery shroud — huzza ! —
   And I bend the bellowing sail.

The woodland note is sweet to hear
   And soft the hum of hives ;
But there 's no music to my ear
   Like that which Ocean gives
When speeds our bark, with every spar
   Taut strained her flight to urge,

Mid rattling tramp and wild huzza,
   We breast the battling surge.

They say the landsman's bosom thrills
   With deeper joy than ours,
That glory crowns the sunset hills,
   And fragrance scents the bowers;
But off! stretch seaward from the bar!
   Spread out the canvas free, —
And should he hail, cry back — "Huzza!
   Our home is on the sea!"

THE NEGLECTED OPPORTUNITY;
OR, THE VISIT OF FORTUNE.

WEARY with play a gentle boy
   Laid down awhile to rest,
When Fortune came with gifts of joy,
   And bade him choose the best.
"But heed thee, child, choose once and well,
   I move by wizard time, —
A moment, and I weave my spell
   Far in another clime!"

Light in the urchin's glances burned,
   And gladness overmuch,
As one by one each toy he turned
   Beneath his curious touch;
Now *this* contents his changing will,
   Now *that* his eyes pursue,
Pleased he retains the one — until
   Another charms his view.

But as the youth the glittering store
   Surveyed in doubt profound,
The mystic wand which Fortune bore
   Dialed the *moment* round.

True to the time, the maid of Fate
  Fled with her gifts of cost,
And left the boy, to mourn, too late,
  The prize forever lost.

Oh ye of manhood's pondering dreams,
  Whose pulses bound with health,
Waste not your hours o'er idle schemes
  Of speculating wealth!
The course your mind first turned to choose,
  Pursue with steady aim,
And ye shall win when others lose
  At Fortune's fickle game.

IN MEMORIAM.

[ON the occasion of the performance of the Burial Service, according to the Protestant Episcopal Church, over the remains of Francis T. Lyon and Mary his wife, both of whom lost their lives by an accident occurring to the steamer *St. John*, on her trip from Albany to New York, October, 1865.

A day or two only had passed after the celebration of their marriage, when the remains of this unfortunate pair, wrapped in their wedding-clothes, were conveyed again from the bridal church, to repose calmly in the tomb until the last trump should awaken them in another and a better world.]

LAY them gently side by side,
   Bow the head and bend the knee,
Let them, both in life allied,
   Still in death united be!

At the altar's shrine they gave,
   'T was but yesterday, the vow,
Earthly binding to the grave, —
   Let that grave receive them now!

Lowly, slowly place them *here*,
   Closely coffined breast to breast;
Bride and bridegroom ever near, —
   What can harm their future rest?

Where the billows roll and rock,
    Never more shall rush of steam,
Nor the rail-king's thunder shock
    Come to break their placid dream.

Star of hope eclipsed in night!
    Lamp of love gone out in gloom!
Lit by Heaven's Promethean light,
    Ye shall shine beyond the tomb.

Lay them gently side by side,
    Bow the head and bend the knee,
Let them, both in life allied,
    Still in death united be!

THE WINTRY WRECK.

All night along the restless sea
    Was heard the minute-gun,
Where broke upon the rocky lea
    The billows one by one.
Full many a heart with fear misgave,
    And many a cheek grew pale,
As wilder dashed the roaring wave,
    And louder shrieked the gale.

Oh! well might quake the landsman's form,
    Tears flood the landsman's eyes,
When, mingled with the hurtling storm,
    Came sounds of human cries.
The wintry shore rose cold and steep
    Beneath the starlight ray,
While, far beyond, upon the deep
    A bark dismantled lay.

As rose the sun with flame of light,
    But not with warmth of flame,
His buried rays disclosed a sight
    Which Pity weeps to name.

From deck and shroud and icy mast,
   Mid ocean's briny rain,
Hands were outstretched upon the blast,
   Waving for help in vain.

Fathers stood forth with nerves of might;
   Mothers — alas for them!
And ah! the maid whose hair was bright
   With ocean's frozen gem!
The strong grew weak within that ship;
   Strangely the weak grew strong;
And they were there whose rosy lip
   Would breathe no more of song.

In lifelike posture some reclined,
   A stark, stiff, marble form,
No more to hear the warring wind,
   Nor feel the ruthless storm;
While, side by side, — just as they died, —
   Clasped in each other's fold,
In life, in death, the same allied,
   Some slept, serene and cold.

But ho! joy, joy! the life-boat comes!
   Bear up, ye few who can!
Rouse for the rescue as with drums, —
   Battle as man with man!
And they *were* rescued, who outbraved
   That night of fearful cost:
Smiles and kind greetings for the saved!
   Tears for the loved and lost!

GOING HOME.

[AN affecting incident is said to have occurred on board the *Reindeer*, a steamer plying between Albany and New York, soon after an explosion which involved great destruction of life in that ill-fated transport. A little girl, five or six years of age, was laid alongside of her mother, whose spirit was passing in an agony of pain from its earthly tenement. Turning her eyes toward her mother she said, "Mamma, it is getting so dark — will we not be home soon?" It was but a moment after this touching expression, that the film was lifted from the eyes of the little sufferer and she *did* go home. She was borne on the wings of angels to the bosom of Him who said, "Suffer little children to come unto me."]

THEY laid her by her parent's side,
   Where she had asked to come;
"Mamma! it is so dark," she cried,
   "Will we not soon be home?"

And did the birdling deem 't was night
   When still the sun was high?
And did her bosom feel affright,
   While *mother* yet was nigh?

Ah! what henceforth was parent dear,
   Or day that brightly shone!
For her no more was sunbeam here,
   No more was mother's tone.

But 't was not long, mid shadows gray,
　　The blind one had to roam;
An angel met the lamb astray,
　　And led the wanderer "*home.*"

THE MERRY SLEIGH.

Jingle! jingle! clear the way,
'T is the merry, merry sleigh!
As it swiftly scuds along,
Hear the burst of happy song;
See the gleam of glances bright
Flashing o'er the pathway white:
Jingle! jingle! how it whirls,
Crowded full of laughing girls!

Jingle! jingle! fast it flies,
Raining shafts from hooded eyes,
Roguish archers, I'll be bound,
Little minding whom they wound.
See them with capricious pranks,
Plowing now the drifted banks:
Jingle! jingle! mid their glee,
Who among them cares for me?

Jingle! jingle! on they go,
Capes and bonnets white with snow,
At the faces gliding past,
Nodding through the fleecy blast;
Not a single robe they fold,
To protect them from the cold:

Jingle ! jingle ! mid the storm,
Fun and frolic keep them warm.

Jingle ! jingle ! down the hills —
O'er the meadows — past the mills —
Now 't is slow, and now 't is fast,
Winter will not always last !
Every pleasure has its time,
Spring will come and stop the chime :
Jingle ! jingle ! clear the way,
'T is the merry, merry sleigh !

THE LOVER'S LEASE.

A HEART to let! a heart to let!
  Who bids? who wants to hire?
A heart which, should your *own* forget,
  Will not with grief expire.
I do not boast its value much;
  'T is filled with vagaries vain,
And, schooled beneath a *practiced* touch,
  Breathes back a practiced strain.

Subject to change, as torrid climes,
  'T is fond of *you* — or *you;*
But then 't will suit these business times
  As well as one more true.
The cheapest chance you'll find by far;
  I'll lease it " less than cost," —
Since constancy is " under par,"
  And love is " labor lost."

A heart! come, bid! be not afraid,
  'T is quite a pleasing toy,
And just the thing for idle maid
  Who wants an hour's employ.

A bargain is this heart of song:
  Bid loud — how much? bid fast;
The lease is just one fortnight long —
  Love swears till then 't will last.

Ding! dong! I cry a heart to hire,
  Almost as "good as new;"
If after fourteen days you tire,
  'T will care not if you do.
But warranted till then — no more —
  Else 't would the world amaze:
Ding! dong! who'll take this heart in store
  For only fourteen days?

THE LOST CREED.

" I love but only you."

Love only you? 'T is asking more,
   Believe me as I live,
Than Constancy has got in store,
   Or Faith knows how to give.
The daisy fair, the tulip tall,
   The lily bright with dew, —
What! slight the whole, — rose, pink, and all, —
   And love but only you?

As fables say, in days of yore,
   When Love with Beauty strayed,
The maid believed the vows he swore,
   The youth believed the maid;
But neither now the book can find
   From which fond trust they drew,
And both have lost from heart and mind
   The creed "I love but you."

Of houri hearts, an hundred score
   Are in the Moslem heaven;
The priest had never less than four,
   The prophet less than seven;

When but for *one* the patriarch prayed,
  Kind fate assigned him *two:*
I'd be afraid, my charming maid,
  To love but only you.

"Still, only you?" Was ever man
  Perplexed like this before?
By Jove! I'll love you all I can —
  And who could promise more?
I'll call you mine — dove, dear, divine;
  But, honor bright and true,
I do declare I dare not swear
  To love but "only you."

LOVE'S PERFIDY.

We meet no more together;
   Yet do not think it strange,
Since Fortune's fickle weather
   Is always fraught with change.
The mists which break at morning
   Are governed by no laws,
And so both you and I, my girl,
   May part without a cause.

If once I had the notion
   Love's wound could never heal,
Such foolish, fond devotion
   No longer now I feel;
Since you have taught that passion
   Is quite a thing of art,
I feel that I've become, my girl,
   A skeptic in the heart.

Your eyes cannot annoy me,
   However bright they glow;
Your words cannot decoy me,
   However smooth they flow;

In sooth, by your example,
   So callous have I grown,
I care not for your smile, my girl,
   Nor do I heed your frown.

The play at length is over
   Before it well began;
I 've acted once the lover,
   And now will try the man;
But not in tragic story,
   To sigh upon the stage;
Nor do I make for you, my girl,
   An "exit in a rage."

THE FOOT-RACE.

Down in a little lane,
Lived a little maid so vain,
So sure she was of beating when she ran, ran, ran;
And this little maiden said,
"Oh, I 'm not the least afraid,
So, little sir, come, catch me, if you can, can, can."

You should have seen the chase,
'T was such a funny race;
A very funny race it was they ran, ran, ran;
The maiden full of laughter,
And, close pursuing after,
As hard as he could tear, the little man, man, man.

More of this little maid
To mention I 'm afraid;
Some other time I 'll tell you, if I can, can, can;
But you may safely bet
They are not running yet —
That maiden and that funny little man, man, man.

RHYMES FOR THE TIMES.

This world is very fanciful,
    And changing all the time, —
While some are fond of politics,
    And some are fond of rhyme.

Patterns are some of piety,
    Of wickedness are some;
One lectures on sobriety,
    Another *treats* on rum.

Some are the soul of honor,
    A blessing where one lives;
Some (on the whole) have little soul,
    Except what money gives.

Some will rebuke you rudely,
    Yet be your friend the while;
While some will smile before your face,
    And "stab you while they smile."

Some are in love with gambling,
    Some are in love with girls;
Some "hide their talents in the earth,"
    Some cast to swine their pearls.

www.ingramcontent.com/pod-product-compliance
Lightning Source LLC
Chambersburg PA
CBHW020242240426
43672CB00006B/614